NO ACTING PLEASE

ERIC MORRIS AND JOAN HOTCHKIS

**Ermor Enterprises
Publishing**

ACKNOWLEDGMENTS

With gratitude to Daniel Spelling for the tireless efforts put forth in editing the text. For him it was truly a "labor of love."

And to Paul Whitehouse for his insight and encouragement in the publication of "No Acting Please."

And to all the actors who were instrumental in the evolvement of the techniques herein.

Eric Morris

Joan Hotchkis

Also by Eric Morris

Irreverent Acting
Being and Doing
Acting from the Ultimate Consciousness
Acting,Imaging and the Unconscious
Coming soon: The Diary of a Professional Experiencer

Audio Tapes

The Craft of Acting
The Megapproaches
Imaging for Acting

**For further information on Eric Morris,
his work, the books and audio tapes visit
our web site: www.ericmorris.com**

The Eric Morris Actors Workshop is located at:

5657 Wilshire Blvd, Suite 110, Los Angeles, CA 90036
(323) 466-9250

If you find the information in this book valuable, you'll be interested to know that cassette tapes by Eric Morris are now available. These 60- to 90-minute audio tapes were recorded live at actual workshops and seminars conducted by Mr. Morris and are ideal for use in conjunction with all his books. The tapes are offered in a series covering the entire system of work, but each separate tape is a complete and exciting learning tool by itself.

To receive the first tape plus a full information brochure, send your check for $9.95 plus $1.00 for postage and handling to:

Ermor Enterprises
8004 Fareholm Drive
Los Angeles, California 90046

Money refunded if not satisfied.

FOREWORD

Eric and I met as students in the sense memory class he describes in this book. No one was more zealous in pursuit of "the work" than "the manic-depressive dane." Nothing daunted Morris. Not the actress who really fainted in "Dark of the Moon"; not the actor who wore rubber bands and couldn't figure out from which side of his mouth to spit his Ludens cough drops; not me as the nazi of your dreams driving him quivering and vulnerable through the concentration camp of his; not even being called the most pretentious ass this side of Sasha Guitry at four a.m. by some angry young actor with Gallo on his lips. Eric was always helpful to others, and most important to himself.

The reality is no one can tell you how to act. My own feelings and observations tell me it requires deep personal commitment to allow any individual to move from that vague desirous state of "I'm gonna be an actress (or actor)" to a point where the actor has some vague sense that every part in which he is cast is not some incredible piece of luck like saying the secret word on "You Bet Your Life," but the result of some solidly acquired skills which, in there, where the truth is, he can call his own.

No book is going to contain all of the things which have helped other actors arrive at a free use of their talent.

As is pointed out in this book, many people feel any academic approach to acting is in conflict with the "Gypsy," or intuitive element of this craft. I suppose the reason Eric asked me to write something for the front of this book is because we have been in many classes, workshops, groups, whatever, together where we observed an experienced talent struggling for agonizing, tedious, and hysterical periods of time to break through and become expressive. If you're interested in this sort of thing, it can be an inspiring process. It's not for everyone. It's not "entertaining," though it can be. There are no guarantees or diplomas, but it can be deeply satisfying to acquire and be a part of another's acquisition of the tool which allow them to enjoy and express their talent.

The concept of "Being" as opposed to "Acting" is Eric's focus here. Along the way he describes exercises related to actor's adversary number one, Tension; relating, stimuli, levels of consciousness, behavior, vulnerability, unpredictability, specificity, and many others. What is described has worked in some way for one actor or another. The Method is, "If it works, use it."

— **Jack Nicholson**

CONTENTS

3. Common Sensory Acting

4. Preparation

Members of a class concentrating on reaching their feelings before a Being exercise at Eric's retreat.

1

BEING

ON *BEING*

Acting is the art of creating genuine realities on a stage. No matter what the material, the actor's fundamental question is: "What is the reality and how can I make it real to *me*?" In this kind of training the actor discovers himself fully both on the stage and off, since the exercises in this book repeatedly demand an integration of living and acting. It is a way of life, not just a way of work.

For the first few years I taught acting to the letter. I was faithful to the Stanislavsky-derived techniques I had learned and my approach to creating realities on the stage encompassed sense memory, affective memory, task choices, etc. Over this period I became increasingly aware that some actors could use the work quite well and other actors, also talented, couldn't make it happen. It didn't work for them. Even for the actors who did well, there remained huge areas unreachable to them and their work often seemed clinical and academic. I became frustrated. I began to doubt "The Method" as a total approach, began to believe the pessimistic sayings of the master acting teachers, that only two percent of actors could use "The Method." And even in my own work as an actor I was frustrated, disappointed in the results I was getting. It was about this time that I started asking some questions, such as how can the same technique work for everybody. Not everybody is the same. We all have different fears, different inhibitions, a variety of different concerns and certainly different backgrounds. Why are actors afraid to talk about themselves personally? Why do acting teachers shy away from discussing the personal elements in acting? Why is everybody so secretive?

I came to the realization that while there's lip service paid to using your personal life on stage and getting "deep" into your own emotions, few actors have the courage to do this and most teachers aren't even aware of the necessity for this kind of search. You can't teach a man to run if he hasn't got legs. Nor can you teach a person to act if he isn't connected to his inner self. I started to develop an approach to acting which embarked on a search of the *self* and led toward usage of the *self* on stage. Out of this approach came a whole system of work which included some of the skills of "The Method," but these skills now became really applicable because they were emanating from a really personal nucleus. I discovered that one of the reasons why many actors couldn't use the Stanislavsky system was because of the separation between technique and personal reality. How can a system designed to be personal work for actors who are not personal and don't even know what they feel?

I invented exercises which required that actors search for their own personal points of view about everything and express it. Hundreds of exercises evolved out of working with actors who were struggling with individual problems. Some of these exercises are named after the actors they were first designed for, although later, of course, they applied to other actors. The "Rounds" were born. I demanded that actors encounter each other in Reluctancy Exercises, in Honesty Stream of Consciousness, in Ego Reconstructions and other Round Exercises. (We'll describe all of these later.) I encouraged them to be extremely personal with each other, to do away with their social impositional life and to experience the *real moment* no matter what the imagined consequences.

At first it was unsettling. People offended each other. People walked out of class, broke down and cried, became hysterical. But something important started to happen to these actors that had never happened in their work before. A kind of visceral reality superseded their concerns about how they looked, how they sounded, or how the scene "should go." I started to see the real people in the scenes, as they were when they weren't acting. People were beginning to BE, at first only in brief moments here and there, but the difference between BEING and *acting* was glaringly obvious to all of us. Once the actors had tasted these moments of BEING, their appetites were whetted for more. Both actors and audience became dissatisfied with less than the truth.

In my classes I urged each actor to do the most difficult thing first, because then all the less difficult problems were done away with in one fell swoop. For example, a girl would come into class very uptight, very proper, possibly with parochial school background, wanting desperately to act, but paralyzed with her concern about being a nice girl. The first exercise I'd give her might be a Vulgarity or perhaps a Sensuality or an Anti-Social. If it was a Vulgarity, I'd ask her to stand up in front of the class and be crude, vile, pick her nose, scratch her ears, belch, use profanity, put her hand on her crotch. All of these things would be overwhelmingly difficult for her to do. But even if she would do part of these, the ice was cracked. The class would accept and encourage her and the atmosphere was permissive, supporting her awareness that she has the right to do these things and it's okay. After this one exercise, the actress might be freed of a whole cluster of social mannerisms which had stood between her and her real feelings.

The results of these Therapy Exercises were amazing. What in my first five years of teaching had remained a persistent problem with the student was now alleviated immediately and in several months didn't exist. The solving of problems like this allowed us to get deeper into the rich life which lay beneath. In the process of discovering themselves, the actors became aware of not only how they felt on a moment-to-moment basis here and now, but also of the scores of things that had affected them throughout their lives. Now we were no longer just using sensory choices that sounded good and usable in a scene. The sensory choices had become more personal and private and affecting. We were beginning to touch the nucleus of the individual self. A more personal and exciting reality began to exist on the stage in the framework of a scene, not consistently at first, but with continued work, more and more. Often in class I would give an actor a "Jellybean" which is a statement, a thought, or a concept designed to pinpoint specifics, or inspire the actor to think in a certain area of craft or personal concern. Sometimes a simple three word "Jellybean" would take the place of a long-winded critique, and zero in on the overview of the entire problem.

 **JELLYBEAN:**

No Acting, Please

I must define at this point what I mean by BEING. It is not a word I chose accidentally. It came to me from working with actors who were trying to achieve that state of life on stage which was the fullest, the most real and the most total. This state usually occurred when they would get closest to what they really felt, and farthest from their customary "acting." When they were closest to what they really felt, their behavior on stage included all kinds of life, infinite colors, distractions, interruptions and unpredictable changes of emotions. Even the identifiable emotions—anger, hate, love, fear—had more facets when they came out of this kind of reality. When an actor in a scene attempts to achieve a particular emotion, what usually occurs is that his presentation of that emotion is flat and one-dimensional. I refer to this phenomenon as "on the nose" acting. It happens because the actor is concerned with delivering the result "on the nose," so consequently the emotion doesn't contain all the elements from which it came, the sources, the impetus which caused the emotion in the first place. When the actor is functioning from a BEING state, all that he feels is included in the life being expressed, and then the resulting emotion contains all of his own personal truth and reality.

When commenting upon an actor's work, telling him or her it was fuller and more believable, I'd invariably get the response, "But Eric, I didn't do anything! I was just being me! What about the theatrical demands?" Ironically, when the actor would approach the BEING state, he'd become much more theatrical and he'd meet the demands of his material on a more complex and imaginative level, because more kinds of life, more subtleties of reality were going on. The exciting thing about successfully achieving BEING on stage or in front of the camera is that it stands out like a beacon in the night. The actor brings to his work the undeniable uniqueness of himself and the work takes on a personal quality that has a fabric incomparable to anyone or anything else. It is unpredictable to the actor. It is filled with inspiration and surprises which eliminate conventional expectations. It has a crisp "one time" feeling that actually makes the audience believe it is happening here and now for the very first time, because, in a sense, it really is.

The craft is not designed to be an esoteric laboratory involvement, but an applicable approach to achieving the most exciting life possible. In the last analysis, if it doesn't produce results, it is only good sounding philosophy.

BEING is a state you work to achieve. To BE you must find out what you feel and express it totally. Let one impulse lead to another without intellectual editing, including all the life that is going on— the interruptions, interferences and distractions. These elements should all be included in the behavior. *Do no more or less than you feel.* BEING is the only place from which you can create organic reality.

TAPED EXCERPT
FROM *BEING* EXERCISE

The scene: A class for professional actors at the Eric Morris Acting Workshop in Hollywood. Everyone is seated in the theatre seats. The stage is bare except for a chair in the center. Eric says, "E.J., get up there." E.J. walks on stage. She is a musical comedy actress known for her soubrette-ingenue roles on stage and television. The following dialogue was taken from a tape of the class session.

Eric: All right. I want you to sit in the center of the stage and BE. Do no more or less than what you feel.

E.J. sits down on the chair and begins to pull herself together. She sits up straight, smiles winningly at the audience, folds her hands in her lap. She is getting ready to present the best part of herself to the world.

Eric: What are you doing?

E.J.: What do you mean, what am I doing?

Eric: How do you feel?

E.J.: What do you mean, how do I feel?

Eric: You're doing things on stage that have nothing to do with what is.

E.J.: Well, I'm nervous. I feel a little shaky. You've got me upset.

Eric: Okay.

E.J.: I don't like to be picked on.

Eric: You're not being picked on.

E.J.: The hell I'm not. I know what you're doing.

5

Eric: Okay. I think you're angry and I think you're suppressing it and functioning in spite of it. You're hostile and defensive and you're functioning above that.

E.J.: Yes, I am.

Eric: That's not BEING. That's not BEING at all. That's "I'm BEING in spite of myself." What's that? That's not BEING.

E.J.: Well, I don't know what the hell you want me to do, Eric! You told me to sit here and I'm trying to sit here!

Eric: Okay. Do you want to cry now?

E.J.: (Starting to cry) No!

Eric: It's not pure.

E.J.: (Sobbing) Stop it!

Eric: Stop what?

E.J.: (Sobbing and screaming) I felt so great coming into this lousy class!

Eric: You do this, one, to avoid finding out what's going on and, two, to get yourself off the spot and, three, to get out of dealing with what you have to deal with. You still aren't BEING. You're closer because you've expurgated a little shit. How do you feel?

E.J.: I feel great. Thanks. I really do. I mean I'm so tired. I worked all day, I earned—earned a lot of money this week and I'm tired. I didn't even want to come tonight, but I did. Because I love to come here and be spit upon!

Eric: Is that what you think we're doing?

E.J.: No, I'm teasing. I know what you're doing Eric . . . Somewhere. I don't know . . . (crying a little). And BEING— I mean—just BEING—I'm trying to figure it out.

John (a student): You can't figure it out.

Eric: Maybe you shouldn't try to figure it out. Maybe you

6

should just find out how you feel. So far you've told us what you did this week and about coming here tonight—

E.J.: (Yelling)   Well, I felt all right, Eric, before I got here!

Eric: What makes you think that you don't feel all right now? Because -

E.J.: Because—

Eric: Does all right mean this as opposed to that? What does all right mean?

E.J.: It means all right.

Eric: All right means everything. You're still not doing the exercise. You're avoiding and evading, evading and avoiding. You know how you get to BE? You get to "How do I feel now and am I functioning in terms of how I feel now? If not, why not and what can I do to get to that?"

E.J.: My hands are shaking.

Eric: You took your glasses off. You keep maintaining that you can't see and then you take your glasses off so that you won't see.

E.J.: (Laughs)

Eric: Does that protect you?

E.J.: Will you wait until I finish wiping my eyes, okay?

E.J. puts her glasses on and looks out at the audience.

Eric: How do you feel?

E.J.: Nervous.

Eric: Okay. Let's see it.

E.J.: I don't know what to do!

Eric: Admit it.

E.J. I just did!

Eric:	Where are you nervous?
E.J.:	My hands are shaking. (She holds them in her lap.)
Eric:	Let us see that. Share that. How can you BE if you want to hide? You're looking at the floor now. Now that you've got your glasses on and can see, you don't want to see. You know why? Because you want to avoid the responsibility of feeling the feedback. *Deal* with the feedback.
E.J.:	You mean the looks I'm getting from the people?
Eric:	And the involvement in the people and the moment-to-moment changes and everything.
E.J.:	Everything . . . and say what I see coming out of them, right?
Eric:	Just BE. Feel what you feel, communicate what you feel, experience what you feel, allow what you feel.
E.J.:	(Starts to cry) I'm looking at Morty and I feel like crying.
Eric:	Why do you feel the responsibility to explain that to us? If you feel like crying, cry! Look at Morty and cry! Don't tell me about it. That isn't BEING.
E.J.:	(Sobs louder)
Eric:	Why are you crying now, because I'm yelling at you?
E.J.:	No. No, it's not because you're yelling at me.
Eric:	What is it?
E.J.:	(Sobs and says something incoherent)
Eric:	Okay. Let it run its course. Don't cover your mouth. That's not BEING. Let it run its course and maybe it'll give way to something else. Don't cut it off. Let it happen. Let it run its way out.
E.J.:	(Sobs even louder with prolonged moans)

Eric: You know, I don't believe you. You're doing everything
           except what I'm asking you to do. Almost all of your
           hostility and defensiveness and all of your crying is some-
           thing which is self-stimulated, something that you
           encourage to happen.

E.J.:   Oh, fuck, Eric! I felt so great when I walked in that door
           tonight!

Eric: Now wait a minute, wait a minute. Let's iron out what
           you mean by I felt so great. Do you mean now you feel
           terrible?

E.J.:   (Sobbing) Well, I really feel shaky.

Eric: As opposed to what? . . . Listen to me.

E.J.:   I am, Eric!

Eric: Why do you feel the necessity to be defensive? I'm not
           attacking you. I'm trying to help you.

E.J.:   I know you are.

Eric: Do you believe that?

E.J.:   Yeah, I do.

Eric: Okay, fine. I think that you function on a level which is
           above BEING. *Beyond* BEING. It is a level of social obli-
           gation. I think you are enormously affected by social
           obligation. Therefore, when social obligation is heightened
           by the presence of people and the obligation to see and
           be seen, you feel the necessity to *do.* And when that is
           frustrated, the only thing you then can do is to cry, to feel
           upset and frustrated and anxiety-ridden. And that ex-
           presses itself in a single way—the way you saw it tonight.
           But your expression isn't pure. It comes out of frustra-
           tion and instead of being frustrated and expressing that,
           you go to the crying and yelling because that expurgates
           the tension, the anxiety of being on the spot. It alleviates
           your confusion and it fulfills an element which is very
           important to you: meeting the social obligation. You
           have been doing what you think people expect of you for so

long that you don't know what *you* expect of yourself or how to get it. When the social obligation is a big question mark, as it is to you in this exercise, you function on a level which you think is interesting—theatrically attractive. You function on a level of life which feels more secure to you than stopping that indulgence and finding out what the component parts of E.J. are. Now I interrupted you constantly for one very important reason: I wanted you to know from the outset what you do and don't do to find out what you feel, who you are, and what's going on here and now. Every single time I pinned you, you responded the same way—crying or defensive yelling, instead of really allowing yourself to be hurt, openly confused, afraid, helpless, whatever—and allowing those impulses to express themselves moment to moment. Do you know what I mean by BEING?

E.J.:   I do now.

Eric: Okay. BEING is "I'm sitting here, I'm looking around the room, I feel boring and dull and that's okay. I'm crossing my legs. I'm beginning to feel a little self-conscious. All these people are looking at me."

E.J.:   You mean BEING is like a stream of consciousness?

Eric: It can be. It can be anything that is. I'm just doing this out loud to demonstrate, but you don't have to do it out loud. You don't have to open your mouth, unless you're impelled to. (Continuing the demonstration) "I feel a little tension creeping into my neck. Hello, tension. I know you're there. Everybody's looking at me expectantly and I feel like I should do something. That lump in my stomach tells me to do something quick. But I don't have to do anything." That's BEING. Whatever is, is. All right, how do you feel?

E.J.:   Confused. Totally confused.

Eric: Good. I see that.

E.J.:   What's good about being confused? The way I feel right now I couldn't say three lines in any script.

Eric: That's okay. For right now. But you're better off now instrumentally than when you got on the stage.

10

A Being class.

E.J.:   What's that supposed to mean?

Eric: All right, let me be a little presumptuous, E.J., and say that had I given you a piece of material when you first walked up on the stage, you would have read it *well.* But this is not a reading class. I am convinced that I would have been able to predict every movement, every sound, every expression you made. However, if you were to continue the life that's going on now in you and *include* it in that piece of material, I'm sure I wouldn't be able to begin to predict or anticipate what you would do.

John: Yeah, but Eric, if she went with the life that is right now in her and the obligation of the material was to be confident, maybe secure, demure, the perfect hostess, wouldn't the existing life be wrong for the material?

Eric: Sure. But that's the point at which you *begin.* That doesn't mean that the life she's experiencing is right for the material, but from this state of confusion, she can work for a choice stimulating the reality that would make her feel the way she wants to feel for the material. This confusion, this anxiety she's feeling, is the bedrock here-and-now reality. It can be changed to another kind of here-and-now reality, whereas the state she assumes is an unaffectable state.

E.J.:   Oh! So this is just getting ready? Preparation?

Eric: Exactly. Acting is almost all getting ready, because if you're ready and prepared to act, then you can.

11

JELLYBEAN:

Before Acting Must Come Being

The BEING exercise you have just read, whether the actor does it by himself or in a group, is different each time because each actor's true state of BEING and the things he does to avoid BEING are unique. The success of the exercise as demonstrated by E.J. and me depends on the skill and experience of the teacher or director. The BEING exercise could become a mind-manipulating weapon in the hands of a teacher or director who does not fully understand the work and who has not himself experienced it. I take responsibility for manipulating E.J., second-guessing her and leading her into certain areas because, after fifteen years of teaching experience, I am able to ascertain the difference between creative manipulation and destructive manipulation. The motives of the teacher and his perception of knowing *what* to say and *when* are crucial factors and make all the difference.

The craft of acting is the art of BEING and there are many techniques and literally hundreds of exercises to help you accomplish this state of BEING. We hope that in the following chapters you will be able to learn and use these exercises and include them in your own approach. It's not something that happens overnight. You have to practice daily. You have to find a system that works for you. That happens by experimentation, by looking around, going to different teachers, and testing the techniques for yourself.

Most actors learn to act by imitating other actors. By the time you've had fifteen or twenty years of watching actors on a screen or stage, you've acquired a whole unconscious repertoire of mannerisms and things to do. We usually emulate those we admire, but this kind of emulation is dangerous for actors, because you end up externally doing things that come from other actors and these imitations rob you of finding out who you are and what you have to contribute. You're as individual as your fingerprints and individuality is what you have to contribute. You are not only the best thing you have, you're the only thing you have.

Unfortunately, among actors and actresses, there's a stigma against hard work. Many cling to the myth that they can get by on their talent alone without knowing their craft—the delusion of theatrical immortality. Others believe that to study the craft will actually spoil their talent by interfering with "natural instincts." Others depend precariously on rabbits' feet, making the sign of the cross before going on stage, never whistling in the dressing room, vitamin B-12 shots, honey and hot lemon juice, uppers, downers and grass. Some of these things may make you feel good, but none of them help you to act.

An actor must take a stance somewhere. He must decide at what level of creativity he wants to function and then use his time at the cost of success for a while, if need be, and in the face of ridicule. He must find and apply a craft until he makes it a habit, and a very dependable one. Most of the exercises have become vital techniques for *acting* therapy. Acting problems are often life problems. If you have difficulty exposing some aspect of yourself off-stage, you'll have even greater difficulty exposing it on stage. Often an acting problem cannot be solved without changing something in the actor's life.

People come into the profession of acting crippled by all the taboos of our society, rules made by parents, schools and churches. All of these restrictions are anti-BEING: "Children should be seen and not heard . . . Don't talk back . . . Stop daydreaming, you're wasting time . . . Be nice . . . Men don't cry . . . Nice girls don't do that . . ." And thousands of other instructions which insidiously corrode your freedom. As an actor you must spend the bulk of your time in the training process finding and freeing yourself.

What stops us from BEING? Consequences. Fear of ridicule. Rejection. Violation of our "image." Longevity and position ("I've been acting so long I should be able to do more than I'm doing right now, so I have to promote the image that I'm better off than I am"). Age "I'm too old for this experimental stuff"). Fear of failure.

Loosely defined, talent is the ability to be affected by an enormous number of things and to express imaginatively the fullness of everything you feel. But because of social pressures, we as actors have learned to accept only the positive elements of our talent and deny the negative elements. And you must not do that. As a creative instrument you cannot say, "This is okay and it's all right for me to feel that and expose that, but this other thing is not okay and it's not all right for me to expose that." You can't do this because what happens is that you short-circuit your instrument. If you sit there and say to yourself, "I'm not going to show anybody what's going on underneath," you've put a capper on everything you do. One expression leads to another and the minute you stop any one impulse, the flow of your BEING stops. Most people fail at the opening gun. I can tell if an actor is functioning in ten seconds, as soon as he gets up from where he's sitting. One can see either the inclusion of what's going on or the suppression of it, either the presence of life or the absence of life. Most actors are in trouble the moment they begin. The whole concept of BEING—BEING BEFORE DOING—BEING BEFORE ACTING—is based on the acknowledgment, the acceptance and the expression of everything you feel.

Most people think of emotions as negative or positive. They place a value judgment on "nice" or "not nice" emotions, "bad" feelings and "good" feelings. But I don't believe there is anything negative or positive about what you feel. As we often say in class "Everything's a Number Six." I arbitrarily chose the number six; it could be a number eight. The point of choosing any number is to say that all emotions have equal value and no singular emotional response has more emotional value than the last. At auditions most actors choose highly volatile material through which to demonstrate their wares. Very few actors decide on simple scenes. The reason for this is the misconception that the stronger emotions are more important. I'm a sensitive, vulnerable, highly volatile human being. Those are the positive elements of my talent. The same things that make me sensitive and vulnerable and volatile also make me insecure, anxious, depressed, tense and hostile. The same elements that affect me positively also affect me negatively. So I come into the producer's office. He's casting a film. Do I say to him, "I'm a sensitive, vulnerable, volatile instrument, but I'm also depressed, insecure, and anxious"? No, I can't say that to him. I don't want him to see my depression and fear. So I hide it. And the minute I hide something, suppress anything, I hide it all. And then I'm not functioning.

So what do I do instead? I walk in and sit down and instead of getting into Gee-what-great-weather-we're-having-and-how-heavy-the traffic-was-coming-in-from-the-Valley, the producer says to me, "How are you?" And I might say, "Well . . . not so good at this moment. I feel a little tense, because I haven't worked in a long time and I'd like to get this job and I'm afraid to even tell you that because you might think I'm too insecure to do it, even if you hired me. Except that to really show you who I am, so you can see my talent, I have to start from how I'm feeling at this moment."

Using this approach, you might alienate fifty per cent of your prospective employers. But the other fifty per cent, the lovers of truth, will respond to you because out of the usually phony interview you will have created a meaningful moment. In this sense, the cripples might really be the long distance runners. If you expose your limitations and let people see them, you no longer have anything to hide. You're functioning on a level of reality and from a level of reality, you can be creative. From a level of phony bullshit you cannot create anything. Once you've established your state of BEING and you're functioning in terms of what is, you are now ready to deal with the author's intent and the obligations of the material. You will find and execute a choice to bring you to the state of life that the material demands. In other words, you go from your existing state of BEING to that state of BEING required by the material.

 JELLYBEAN:

If You Start With An Empty Blackboard, You Can Write Anything On It

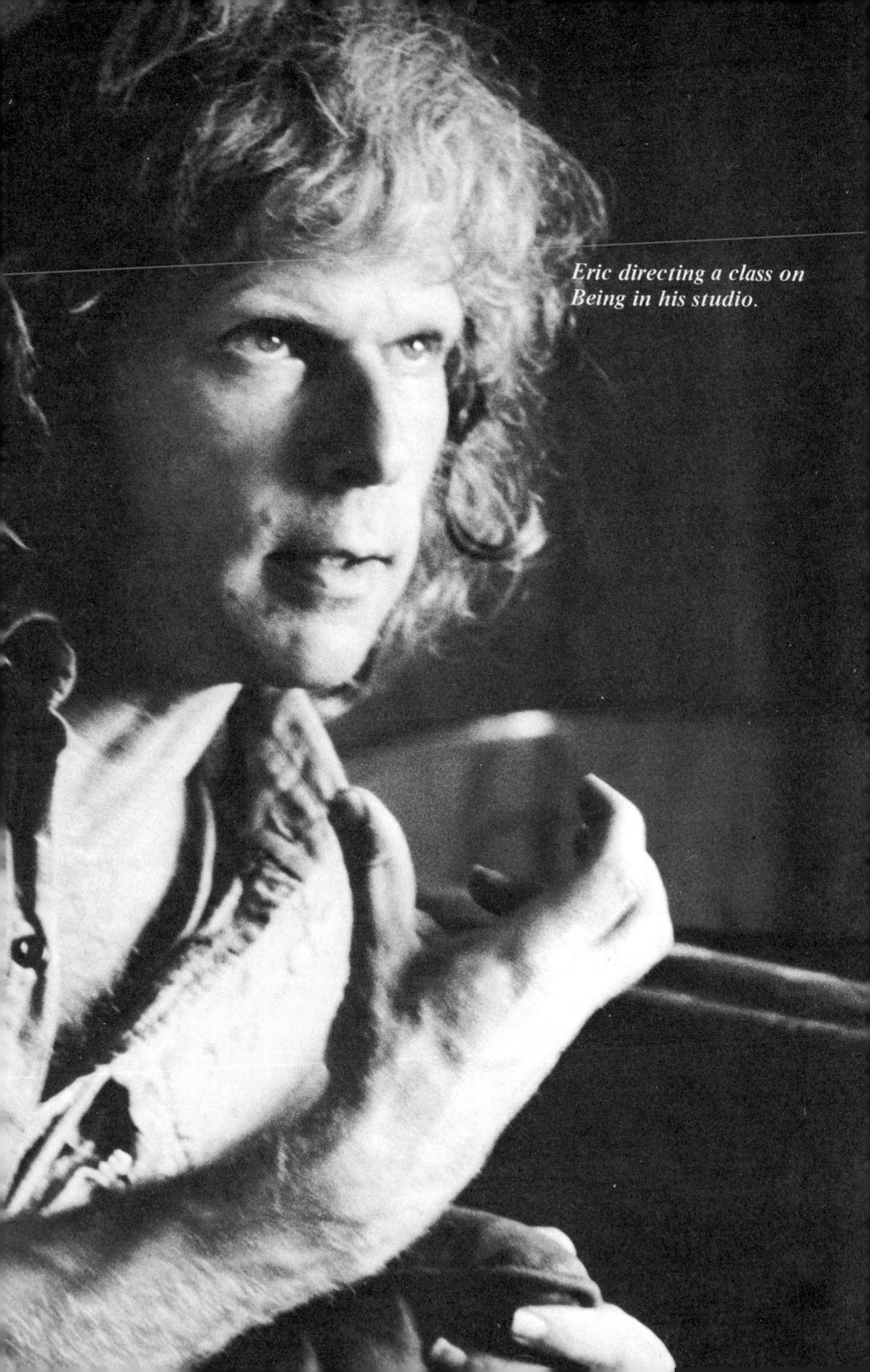

Eric directing a class on Being in his studio.

FROM JOAN'S JOURNAL, 1970:
FIRST CONTACT WITH *BEING*

I'd studied several years with two of the finest acting teachers in the country, Sanford Meisner and Lee Strasberg. I was a hard-working student, dedicated to the method I was being taught. Sandy and Lee teach quite differently, but they shared in common a belief that it wasn't sound professional training to expose your personal choices to the class or talk about your personal life. They kept saying things like, "Don't tell us about that. That's too personal . . . You must try not to be so anxious . . . Don't tell us your choice. It will dissipate it for you." For years my work was stuck on an academic level. It was labored and impersonal and all the techniques showed.

When I first came into Eric's classes, I was repelled by the lack of privacy—actors talking about their mothers and fathers in intimate detail, weeping or howling with glee or smashing the air with their fists—actors sitting around in a circle while each one tells the thing he is most reluctant to reveal—actors cradling each other like babies, crooning lullabies. It looked like an insane asylum to me. I was terrified. I thought if I gave away my secrets, threw them into the public pot, my few treasures would be lost forever and then my acting would be even emptier and drier than it was. But Eric kept saying, "That's mystical bullshit. What are you, a one-choice actress? A three-choice actress? Your life is full of experiences! You're rich with choices!"

I knew down to my bones I'd find the missing link in this kind of training. And I did. And soon. I found the connection to myself. All those personal feelings and fantasies which had been locked out of my work began to flood in. The few choices I'd been using again and again multiplied—miraculously bloomed into countless others. The techniques I'd learned before—improvisation, sense memory, personalization, affective memory—were made much more specific and personal so that I could really depend on them to ignite my work, and, paradoxically, the more skilled I've become, the less the skill shows, which proves what Eric often says, "The craft is designed to do away with itself."

Joan Hotchkis

16

JELLYBEAN:

The Unconscious Is Where Your Talent Lives

The scene: The Professional Class at the Eric Morris Actor's Workshop. Connie and Danny have just finished a scene. They've explained what they were working for and now they're waiting for the critique. Connie is an experienced actress in her early forties, doing her first scene in class tonight. Danny is an attractive young actor, a student in the class for two and one half years. At the moment he is agitated and dissatisfied with his work.

Eric: How do you feel, Connie?

Connie: I feel okay.

Eric: How do you feel, Danny?

Danny: Oh God, Eric, I feel constipated.

Eric: That's okay. (Turns to class sitting in the theatre.) All right, what would anybody like to say?

(Comments from the actors lasted about a half hour. For the most part they were supportive and critically constructive. Part of each actor's growth depends on his ability to perceive and articulate the process of work.)

John: Well, it was a pretty good first scene. I mean, you know, it's not easy to get up there and do a first scene. I'm talking about Connie now. What I really feel about her work, Eric, is that it was too general. (Class protocol requires

17

that you talk to the actor through Eric. Direct criticism often provokes two-way conversations which can lead to defensiveness and then the points are lost.) She said she "personalized" her sister, but I didn't see that. How did she work for that? She said she had an "intention" of seducing Danny, but as far as I could tell, she was too self-involved to even see him. I didn't see any relationship between them at all. And her lines—uh—they just sounded like lines, not like talk. As for Danny, I liked a lot of what he did. I think Danny has a tendency to make trouble for himself. He comments on what he's doing instead of allowing it just to be. He's too hard on himself. But I must say I see more and more of Danny every time he does a scene here.

Savannah: I don't altogether agree with John about Connie. I mean, my God, I saw such wonderful underlying sensitivity. I don't want Connie to leave here tonight without knowing how special I feel she is. I saw moments of real need and loneliness that—well—she really touched me. I agree with John that she has to learn to work with choices specifically, but let us see more of Connie in the work. Connie, you're beautiful. And Danny, will you for Christ's sake let yourself alone? All this self-beating. I mean, I really get tired of it. You don't *need* to do that anymore, Danny. It's all *there* . . .

(About fourteen other people commented, and then Eric gave his critique.)

Eric: Connie, I know exactly how you work from watching this scene. I know that's pompous to say. I haven't seen everything you've done, but I know how you work. Now, it took you 'X' number of years to get as good as you are with what you do. Isn't that true? Would you accept that?

Connie: Yes, I've done a lot of work.

Eric: I can see that. And it's not bad work. It's good. I mean, if somebody walked in off the street and saw you do that scene, they wouldn't say that was bad work. They wouldn't say that girl can't act. Nobody in his right mind would say that. It wasn't great work, but it certainly wasn't bad work. It represented a kind of training and background and it was certainly professional. And it took 'X' number of years to get to that. So if you take 'X' number of years and you say "Okay, I'm going to learn Stanislavsky, Strasberg, Uta Hagen, Eric Morris, Stella Adler, whatever. I'm going to learn that technique." A equals B equals C equals D. All of that is a fixed process insofar as it is a language. But none of it means anything to anybody unless you have a canvas to paint it on. I can come in here and say, "I've just invented the greatest oil colors known to man. Nobody's ever had these colors!" But what do you put them on? You gotta have a canvas. The canvas is you. Your canvas is BEING. Now had you done something else in 'X' number of years, you'd be behaving differently here tonight. If ninety per cent of your time went into BEING and learning how to BE, finding out who you are and what makes you function, and ten per cent went into your "system," your technique or whatever you call it, that would be a proper proportion. The craft of acting can be taught to an idiot in six months. It's not hard. It's very easy. It makes a lot of sense. What's difficult, what gets in the way, are the obstacles to BEING, which are your obligations—theatrical, social and emotional. All your obligations get in your way. That's why we have exercises like I Allow, I Permit, I Accept, Personal Inventory and Double Exposure. The *main* thing is not an acting problem. It's a *living* problem. What you can't allow yourself to feel *out there,* you won't allow yourself to feel here on stage. You can't make a separation between life out there and life on stage. You can't walk out of here tonight and think that you're dealing with an acting problem. You're dealing with a living problem. There isn't anything you cannot do on the stage. You might be wrong. You might go out in left field, and even throw the play, which isn't what I'm recommending. But I would love to go to the theatre and take the chance of having an actor throw the play because of his courage, his risk-taking, than to see a predictable, staid, conventional performance. I'd like to go see Tennessee Williams and have the second act suddenly be Arthur Miller. That's better than seeing how everybody "does" Tennessee Williams.

You don't work for a choice *parallel* to doing the scene, Connie, which is what you were attempting here. Working for a choice is a process where you ask sensory questions and you let your senses answer and you commit yourself to that process totally even at the cost of the scene until that process bears some kind of behavioral fruit. Then if your behavior is not what you want for the scene, you adjust your choice or find a different choice. You always include everything that is going on. *There is no acting in acting.* When you're acting, you're not BEING. I know as sure as I'm sitting in this chair, Connie, that what you want will happen for you, if you do this kind of work.

Danny, I agree with a lot of the comments about your making trouble for yourself. I could see that you were in trouble. I could see that a lot of your behavior on the stage came out of frustration at not being able to free the things you felt. It's okay to have problems, if the life comes out of them. But I want to talk about walking the fence. You walked the fence between what you felt and what you thought should be there in the scene. You partially included the life that was going on in you and because of that partial inclusion I found you interesting, sometimes compelling and unpredictable. But instead of surrendering yourself to all of your problems and letting the words come totally out of that life, you kept commenting on your inability to fulfill your concept of the scene. You didn't comment verbally, but I could see your comments. Had you embraced those comments instead of putting them in parentheses, they would have merged into the character's life and since this character is laced with problems and frustrations anyway, you would have had it all going for you. That's what I mean by walking the fence.

You were closer to BEING than Connie was, because I saw more of Danny and I want to make a very important point about this. And that is, as I told Connie, if somebody had walked into this class tonight and seen the work, they would have seen an enormous contrast between you and Connie. She was smooth, polished, certainly professional, whereas you were erratic, filled with problems, somewhat anti-social in your exclusion of the audience. Bumpy. Your work was bumpy and hers was smooth, and I'm sure the person watching would have concluded that she was functioning well as an actress and you were not. We've learned to accept slick acting through conditioning. We see polished work on TV and films and stage and that's what we learn to expect. But when an actor is functioning organically and honestly, he is anything but smooth. He might even look somewhat "unprofessional"–untechnical, undisciplined, untrained. This system of BEING that we're struggling to reach here is often ridiculed, because the approach is unconventional. However, when you are functioning totally from a BEING state, even the severest critics of "Method" work are awed, because the results are anything but conventional. You're truly creating life on stage and people are not smooth in life. They are bumpy, unpredictable, easily derailed, and forget what they were going to say. That's the kind of reality that we as actors want to create on stage.

FROM JOAN'S JOURNAL, 1972:
COMBAT WITH *BEING* OBSTACLES

Wednesday, July 5 . . . . . Performed part of my play in Eric's class tonight and afterwards my good friend, Emilie, who'd come to watch it, said I cry too much and it's wrong for the character of Bissie. I said Eric is directing and at this point he doesn't give a damn about the character. He wants me to find out who I am in relation to Bissie and express all of that. Emilie replied that she thinks my constant tears on stage come out of being too hard on myself and she thinks my self-punitive attitude is a cop-out, because it stops me from really experiencing the realities of what I'm feeling. She said I should take deliberate steps to be kinder to myself, be proud of what I'm doing and accept everything that I am because "everything is everything."

Many times Eric has told me the same thing, that I editorialize as I perform and my inner judgement stops me from BEING.
Emilie's a dancer. Her disciplines are different from ours, but her remarks hit the same bulls eye as Eric's. I'm determined to change this pattern . . .

Saturday, July 29 . . . . . . For three weeks Eric has been away doing a film. I've used the time off from rehearsals to practice my new habit of BEING. I want to get rid of my negative self-analysis, that dubious crutch I've leaned on all my life. So during these three weeks, I've treated myself to all sorts of pleasures. I bought a stereo. I had champagne and peach pie with some friends. I made love. I enjoyed sweet moments with my daughter at the beach. And every time that stern voice inside me said, "You shouldn't be wasting time. You should be working harder. Don't be silly. Don't be greedy. Why are you doing that? Why did you say that?", I deliberately silenced it and continued living . . .

Tuesday, August 1 . . . . . I haven't worked on my play today, but instead of berating myself for that I lay down on the couch and turned my stereo up high. In my head I could hear Eric's voice saying, "Allow! Permit! Accept! Include!" In time to the music. It made me laugh out loud. I went to bed around 10:00 and awoke at 2:30 in the morning with a sensation of unfinished business. Got up, brushed my teeth, made tea and started working on the play. . .

Wednesday, August 2 . . . First rehearsal with Eric since he's been away on the film. He said he saw something he's never seen in my work, a zest for it, a joy and lack of commentary. Then I told him about these three weeks of Non-Judgment Practice and he confirmed that it's having results in my acting already. He said my behavior on stage is more spontaneous and varied than before. There's more creative excitement . . .

DIFFERENT *BEING* STATES

JELLYBEAN:

How You Work In The World Is How You Work On Stage

When you've reached a BEING state, which means BEING where you are at this moment in the here and now, including everything that's going on in you, then you are ready to act. What is meant by the word "act" is to go from your present state of BEING to the state of BEING which the material demands. For instance, your present state of BEING is: "I'm kind of relaxed now, kind of depressed and heavy, looking out of the window, tired and a little down," but the emotional obligation of your material might be a state of excitement and joy, almost euphoria. The character in the play has just been rewarded or has accomplished something and feels very up about it. So you have to find a way to go from *this* BEING state, where you are now, to *that* BEING state. Sometimes

22

the emotional demands of your material are totally opposite to what you're feeling, which gives you an enormous obligation. Many actors fail because they try to jump from *here* to *there* in one step. You might need to move yourself through several interim steps in order to go from your depression to joy.

Using available stimuli around you or working for imaginary choices, you try to find ways to make yourself less depressed and somewhat happier. You might look for things around the room that make you feel better. You might create a certain person in the room who would make you feel very happy. Once you've achieved an interim state of less depression and more happiness, you are ready to influence this interim state though other choices and work toward a higher level of joy. Progressively you encourage one BEING state to give way to another. Sometimes the BEING state you start with is so powerful and has such a grip on you that it's very difficult to affect it. At such times you will realize how important it is to know your instrument thoroughly, to have a large repertoire of choices and the skill to use them to get where you want to go. This ability will come only through hard work and daily practice.

When you are really BEING, one state carries over into the next and influences it like many colors running together and mixing, until your next BEING state becomes the dominant color. You've all seen actors who paint by the numbers, who are laughing one moment and the laughter abruptly stops and you see anger. We call this impositional technique, a symptom of the anti-reality actor. In real life, the moment carries over and mixes with the next moment and you see the emotional subtleties of the change. This doesn't happen unless you're BEING. You must start in the totality of the BEING state, because you cannot create any life on stage or fulfill any scenic obligation until you first have a life going on. You cannot create life from the absence of life.

There's a natural process of responding to life. The process is stimulus-effect-response-expression. First you see, hear, taste, smell or feel something. That's the stimulus. It has some kind of an effect on you. Your instrument responds to that effect. You then express that response. The whole process happens in micro-seconds and it happens over and over again and this is referred to as living, which is BEING. If you are functioning from a BEING state, this natural process goes on without interference. BEING promotes stimulus-effect - response - expression, stimulus - effect - response - expression, stimulus-effect-response-expression.

The actor who premeditates his behavior short-circuits the process anywhere along the line. He is so intent on executing his plan of how the scene should go that the stimulus may not even reach him. Or the stimulus may reach him but he's so committed to his intellectual concepts that he is unaffected by the stimulus. If he's busy simulating an effect, how can he be truly affected? Or he is affected by something that happens on the stage—his partner pats his cheek that night for the first time, but he doesn't allow himself to respond because he's imposing the behavior he feels should be there in the scene. He short-circuits the natural process of life, because he does not include his response to the pat on the cheek. If his responses are exclusive and premeditated, how can he respond with what he really feels? Instead of going with the organic response, his expression becomes prostituted by what he thinks the character should do or say. In this way, one denial sets up a chain reaction of denials until the lack of reality is epidemic.

When the actor short-circuits the natural process by assuming behaviors, by imposing attitudes, by "acting," he creates what are called "splits" in his instrument. There are all kinds of splits—vocal splits, emotional splits, physical and intellectual or any combination of these. The BEING state eliminates the possibility of splits or if the split occurs, BEING mends it.

Even if an actor achieves the BEING state and functions organically, there may be limitations in either the impressive or expressive areas which he needs to work on in order to make his BEING states fuller and more colorful. For instance, actors who are shy and quiet often are extremely imaginative and affectable, but unable to express anything. On the other side of the coin there's the so-called extrovert, the exhibitionist who seems to flow with expression but may not be at all aware or sensitive. This kind of actor needs help in the impressive area, exercises dealing with his vulnerability.

Whatever the actor's problems are (and we all have them at every stage of development), BEING is ground zero. Implicit in BEING is the inclusion of *all* your impulses, including your problems as well as the infinite colors of your emotional rainbow. The denial of even one subtle shade of BEING diminishes your total contribution as an artist. The following exercises all directly relate to BEING. Although these exercises have more than one purpose, they are good ones to begin with, because they are specifically designed to help you to BE.

BEING EXERCISES

1. Personal Inventory I

This is a stream-of-consciousness monologue, which you do semi-audibly, so that you can hear yourself talking, but no one else can. You ask yourself, "How do I feel?" and then you express your feelings and continue to repeat the question. Do it for as little as two minutes or as long as ten minutes and as many times a day as you comfortably can. You can do it at supermarkets, in your car, in a restaurant waiting for a friend, really anywhere. While the exercise is going on, things will interfere with it, interrupt and take your attention away from the process. Include these things verbally in your monologue. For example, "How do I feel? I just cleared my throat, getting ready to do this exercise. I feel obligated to do it. Taking a deep breath. How do I feel? I'm looking for things to grab onto. My eyes are scanning the room. I feel anxious, a little tense in the chest. I hear a fly buzzing in the window. How do I feel? I feel excited about the job I got today. And I feel scared about it, too, starting to work on it. How do I feel? I feel—uh—stuck. I don't know how I feel right now. I feel anxious about not knowing how I feel. That's how I feel! I feel anxious! Taking another deep breath. I feel my stomach is bloated, I wish I could lose weight. I feel a little more in touch with how I feel, a little less anxious. I'm beginning to feel a little excitement rising up . . . wonder where that's coming from? How do I feel? I feel better, etc., etc." Personal Inventory, if practiced regularly, gets you in touch with what you're feeling and trains you to express everything that's going on moment-to-moment. Not every expression is verbal; it might be just vocal, like a sigh or a grunt. It alleviates tension and encourages a state of BEING.

2. One-Person *BEING*

This is a good exercise to use following Personal Inventory. It's not necessary to continue the semi-audible process of asking yourself how you feel. Just *BE!* Allow and permit everything that you feel to express itself vocally, verbally and physically. Acknowledge and include all the obstacles that get in the way of simply going with what is. If, for example, you begin to comment on the propriety of your impulses and start to interfere with the expression of any group of feelings, then you should include your commentary, followed by whatever the true impulses are. The amazing thing about

Just BE!

this process is that one expression gives way to the next and the next after that, and the flow of reality becomes compelling. Do the exercise sitting, standing, lying down or whatever. Simply allow yourself to feel and express anything that's going on. *Try to find your personal gap between obligation and impulse.* Permit yourself to do what you feel and not what you think you should do. For additional ideas about how to do the exercise, refer to the taped dialogue in this chapter between E.J. and myself.

3. Personal Inventory II

The Personal Inventory exercise which we've already described is one of the better ways to become aware of what's going on inside you. You do it many times a day. Get in the habit of finding out how you feel at any given moment. Take inventory of how you're being affected by the objects around you, animate and inanimate. As we said before, you do the exercise audibly or semi-audibly by asking yourself, "How do I feel?" You may add the question, "How do I feel about that?"

After asking yourself, "How do I feel?" and answering the question, your next question should be, "Am I expressing how I feel and if not, why not?" This is an important question to add, because it prevents the exercise from becoming cerebral gymnastics. It turns it into a vigorous learning experience for you. If your answer is, "No, I'm not expressing how I feel," then ask yourself, "What can I do to express it? How can I help myself express my feelings within the framework of the consequence?" For example, "I feel like punching him in the nose. Well, that's consequential to someone else's well-being and to mine, also." When the consequences are too large, you acknowledge your desire to punch that person and you make a conscious choice not to. The element of choice is not as stifling as the element of suppression, stifling the impulse altogether and hiding it from your awareness.

When you're asking yourself, "Am I expressing how I feel and if not, why not?" the WHY is the most important word. The WHY will open up to you the knowledge of the things that stop you from being yourself. "Because I'm afraid of what they will think of me." If that answer keeps coming up, you've got to deal with that as a problem. "Because I don't want them to think I'm less than what I want them to think I am." Once having found the answer to your WHY, you then try to express as much as you can. *You are entitled to all of your emotions.* Nobody anywhere has the right to deny what you feel. You're entitled to the sum total of everything you are. And it's not always nice. It's not always good or social or polite or concerned about others. Sometimes you're loving and giving and you love somebody who is not loving and giving and you're disappointed. You're entitled to that disappointment just as that person is entitled not to love you.

The minute you make rules about what you should feel, those rules carry over to the stage or camera. They carry over because the rules are the conditions by which you live. This doesn't mean you should become an animal and hit people over the head and steal from the Hollywood Ranch Market. That's not what we mean at all. There's a certain level of morality on which people live. But all people have the license to be themselves and we believe that actors have a special license, because feelings are our stock in trade.

4. I Am, I Want, I Need, I Feel

This is done aloud in a stream-of-consciousness fashion, but very rapidly, so that you don't have a chance to reflect on or to premeditate what you say. The purpose is to surprise yourself with what comes out. Start every sentence with one of the four statements, not necessarily in that order. For example: "*I want* to do this exercise . . . *I am* tense . . . *I need* to be good . . . *I need* to be seen . . . *I feel* self-conscious . . . *I feel* my fingers . . . *I need* money . . . *I am* what I am . . . *I feel* foolish . . . *I want* to laugh . . . *I am* laughing . . . *I need* love . . . *I want* to know what I want . . . *I feel* full . . . *I need* space . . . *I am* running out of things . . . *I am* looking at the floor . . . !" The exercise is purposely designed to channel your impulses into the format of "I Am, I Want, I Need, I Feel." When you respond to the specific line of self-questioning, your awareness of the moment-to-moment realities becomes clearer. The important element is the impulsiveness of your response. If you take a beat to think about the response, you might just be filling the blank with your conditioned thought rather than your real feeling. It is important to remember that if you go blank, say the first thing that comes to your mind no matter how illogical or nonsensical it may seem. You may repeat "I Am _____, I Want _____, I Need _____, I Feel _____" many times, but encourage yourself to go back and forth between the four statements.

5. What Do I Want?

The purpose of this exercise is to find out what you want here and now, but also in the larger sense. The exercise differs from I Am, I Want, I Need, I Feel because it is not done impulsively. The reason here is to find out what the underlying life is (i.e., "What do

28

I want in a more complete sense?"). The emphasis is on a more intellectual and philosophical overview of what you want in life. It is necessary to start on a here-and-now level to encourage a free flow and avoid the tendency to become heady. The exercise is done like Personal Inventory, but with the question, "What do I want?" instead of "How do I feel?" For example: What do I want? I want to find out what I want. What do I want? I want to be happier than I am now. I want to work more. I want to be good. I want people to respect me. What do I want? I want not to care about those things. I want to be successful." If you wish, you can include this exercise in the Personal Inventory instead of doing it separately.

The intention of "The Method" is the achievement of organic reality on the stage. All reality on the stage is ostensibly created from the inner life of the actor, from his own living experiences. "The Method" and its inherent techniques are structured to this end; however, the system does not tell the actor *how* this is achieved. Since all people are different and have problems that are unique to themselves, how can any formularized system work the same for everyone? The answer is that it cannot, which is why "The Method" is not widely used or respected. The search and process of finding yourself and achieving a BEING state—that is to say, A STATE OF BEING OURSELVES, TOTALLY, is what this book offers to the actor. BEING is the primary and basic foundation to a creative process. Once the actor arrives at his bedrock reality, the *truth, his* truth, in this moment and at this place, he is ready to effect that truth and change it to anything the material requires. BEING is not a state you achieve immediately, it is a way of life that evolves out of much work and experimentation. Besides requisite ingredients of talent and commitment as an artist, you must have COURAGE. You must be willing to take chances and sometimes suffer the consequences of your actions, to pursue your individuality and to make your statement in life and on the stage. Remember, no one ever contributed lasting things to the world without taking chances and often incurring resentment and controversy from the people around them. Living and acting are all too often separated and they mustn't be. The exercises in this book are specifically constructed to become your tools to bridge the gap between you and your work. The awesome impact of completely BEING on the stage is thrilling to an audience. When you achieve BEING, every part of you knows it! The feeling is unmistakable.

If you use the work prescribed here, practice these exercises daily and make the approach part of your life, you will experience this magical state of BEING. The results of this work are filled with rewards and wonderful surprises.

Karen Gehrman doing a commitment preparation to get loose and ready to work.

Chapter
2

GETTING READY TO GET READY

TENSION:
HOW IT AFFECTS THE ACTOR

According to the dictionary, tension is the act of stretching or straining, being strained to stiffness, a state of tightness, mental strain, nervous anxiety. Without getting into the physiological origins of tension—that's for a medical book— we'll concern ourselves with it as it relates to acting. Tension is a state of BEING that all actors experience and it's usually something that the actor will have to deal with all his life. It manifests itself in thousands of ways, in as many different ways as there are actors. It can be a tightening of the muscles in various parts of the body— back of the neck, shoulders, hands, arms and so forth—sweaty palms, dry mouth, "butterflies," trembling hands, difficulty in breathing, pressure in the chest, and on and on. The actor feels enormously uncomfortable, awkward and self-conscious. These are some of the symptoms of physical tension.

Mental tension affects the actor's thinking. He suffers from either a conglomeration of thoughts and can't remember his lines, or from the absence of thought, the inability to think anything. He is spaced out, stoned, the eyes are vacant, panicked, and there's a tightening around the eyelids. Physical and mental tension usually occur together, both states crippling the actor, making him helpless on stage, incapable of being affected or responding, unable to function on an organic level.

What then can we do with this enemy? Why does it happen? What causes it? And is it completely bad? Or does it have some good aspects? Can it be used? If so, how? These questions and many others will be discussed throughout the book.

Tension is the actor's Number One problem, because unless he knows how to alleviate it, he can't proceed to do anything else. Many actors never get to the nucleus of their real talent because they function above their tension. Tension might be compared to a corked bottle. Let us imagine for a moment that a human being is like a bottle filled with many emotions and impulses. If you were to put a stopper on that bottle, nothing could come out. Tension acts as a stopper and everything below that stopper is trapped and bottled up. The actor then must impose a behavior *above* that stopper and this kind of behavior leads only to intellectual and conceptual acting. You cannot play an idea!

Actors become quite facile at functioning above the cork, never confronting the real life underneath. They develop trademark behavior, elements of "personality," mannerisms that they become well-known for and even hired for. However, in denying their tension and what lies beneath it, they are robbing themselves of ninety per cent of their talent. Their behavior on stage is conceptual, impositional, representational and predictable.

You've all heard actors admit that just before going on stage they experience a lot of tension, but it disappears like magic as soon as they set foot on the boards. If you're one of these actors, we must assume that you become involved at that split second and have gotten rid of your pre-entrance tension. If that's the case, fine. You're in good shape and if it happens that way for you all the time, just skip this chapter entirely.

However, you may be deluding yourself into believing that you're involved. You may have suppressed your tension. You may not even be aware of its presence. This kind of delusion and false sense of well-being is dangerous to you as an actor, keeping you from reaching into the well of your real contribution.

Half the battle in conquering a human problem is first to recognize that it exists. Too many actors deny the existence of tension in themselves. They suppress it so completely that they can only function on a superficial level, a facilitated behavior that can sometimes be quite interesting, but can never be real and organic. You've seen actors who are apparently relaxed. They seem calm and in complete control, but their behavior somehow isn't quite real or believable. They're reacting too broadly perhaps, doing more than they should be doing. Their eyes may be glassed over and they stare at your chin as they speak. This kind of actor, seemingly calm and relaxed, exudes self-confidence all over the stage. You watch him saunter jauntily downstage and pick up a glass or a cigarette and then you suddenly observe that he can't stop his hand from trembling. His knees may also be doing quite a little number of their own. Many actors become adept at suppressing their tension. Through years of experience they've learned to impose a studied naturalness on top of this suppression. These actors are often referred to as competent performers, troupers, pros that go out there and say their jokes and grab their money and run. Competent they may be by some standards, but exciting they will never be!

On the other hand, there's the actor who is all too aware of his tension. He knows he's miserable, but because he doesn't understand his tension or know how to help himself, it cripples him, renders him incapable of working. He literally falls apart. In a field as competitive as the theatre it is detrimental to "show" tension. It may well cost you a job. If you don't show confidence in yourself, *they* won't have confidence in you and they'll get somebody else instead. Therefore, we become conditioned to hiding it and after years of doing just that, we succeed in hiding it even from ourselves.

It is just as easy to *deal* with your tension as it is to impose relaxation. It's simply a matter of redirecting your efforts. You may be thinking at this point, "That's easier said than done." Quite true! It's much easier to talk about dealing with it than actually doing so, but tension is a demon that will be with you your entire life. Don't despair. Tension is also an indication of your talent. It is the manifestation of unexpressed emotions, bottled up impulses, all your personal responses to the world. The more tension you have, the more there is going on inside of you that is not coming out. Tension is the result of an interruption in the natural process of stimulus-effect-response-expression. Your tension is evidence that you are strongly affected by a wide range of stimuli. That's what is meant by the quote "Tension is talent." Usually people with extreme tension problems are people who are extremely sensitive and affectable.

Learning a craft which you can depend on, encouraging a faith in your talent and knowing your own tension problems and how to deal with them are all important factors in your development.

Suppose you go to a doctor for some corrective surgery. He will diagnose the problem, find the right tools to work with and correct the trouble. He will have very little tension about doing his job, because he is sure of his skill and his knowledge of what to do and how to do it. Like the doctor, an actor must also have a craft he can count on. Then, and only then, can he approach his job with the same confidence as the surgeon.

FROM JOAN'S JOURNAL, TUESDAY, APRIL 4, 1972: IDENTIFYING AND DEALING WITH TENSION

First rehearsal with Eric on my play. As I opened my front door for him and said, "Hi," I felt that old knot of fear in my stomach that I used to have for every Broadway audition. It lies near where I breathe and spreads like a fishnet to all parts of my body so that I'm trapped in total self-consciousness.

Eric was his usual self, but I kept reading rejection behind his calm demeanor. That's how I trap myself into that net. I attribute to the director a stream of negative thoughts about me . . . "She's not a good actress, but she looks the part . . . God, what a drag. She doesn't know anything . . . Well, she's neurotic and lonely and getting old. I'll just be patient with her . . . "

There was a time when these negative fantasies polluted almost every piece of work I did. That's how I got fired from my first Broadway musical. From the first day of rehearsal I was convinced the director hated me and the conviction spread through my limbs like blood poisoning. I tripped over the scenery, sprained my ankle, got laryngitis and conjunctivitis until finally, in Philadelphia, he fired me, which my self-hating mind had willed him to do from the beginning.

I didn't know at the time that *tension* was my blood poisoning, the cause of all my maladies. Now, after two years of study with Eric, these cruel fantasies no longer have the upper hand. I know how to help myself. I can get involved in the work now, feel positive and excited about it, even though the dark thoughts still gleam below like dirty water at the bottom of the well.

34

CAUSES OF TENSION

These are examples from Joan's journal of some of the major causes of tension in actors.

1. Joan's anxiety about the "First Rehearsal." (I found in working with her on the play that she had anxiety before each rehearsal. As we worked, it became less.)

2. Her desire to *succeed and be good* in the play.

3. Her lack of specific craft at the time and her lack of faith in the craft she had.

4. Her fear of my judgment and mind-reading negative thoughts into me.

5. Her basic insecurity about being *enough.*

6. Physical manifestations of tension which, themselves, caused more tension.

The causes of tension are infinite. Some of the more common causes are the actor's ego-state, his insecurities, his need to succeed and be good, the fear of failure and the consequences of failing, the absence of craft and the lack of faith in the instrument. The actor's ego-state is very important to his ability to function on stage. If the ego-state is low, he'll have minimal faith in himself and, therefore, maximum anxiety and fear of failure, which leads to tension. When you are at peace with yourself and you feel you're a worthy person with much to offer, then it's much easier to be successful at anything you do and you'll experience much less tension. In fact, it might simply be the pleasant sensation of excitement.

Some actors are in a perpetually low ego-state due to childhood conditioning and other reasons. Other actors who tend to be more confident may at certain times be overcome by life—losing a job, going through a divorce, waking up one morning feeling hopeless about the future. At these moments, if you have to get on stage and act, you'll have a great deal of tension. You can either deal specifically with the tension or with the causes of it—your low ego-state— or with both problems. You'll find in this book a large number of exercises for building a better ego-state quickly. Of course, you seldom can define the exact reasons for a high or a low ego-state and it's not really important to try. What's important is to get your ego to where you want it to be for the work you have to do. Many kinds of ego preparations will be described and you will discover many of your own. As the saying goes, "If it works, use it!"

Talent is an oblique thing made up of many fears, frustrations and unfulfilled desires. Insecurity, another major cause of tension, is bred by these particular elements of talent. Talent is a beautiful gift and has many other wonderful elements but, unfortunately, it can stand in its own way. Everybody on earth has insecurities of one kind or another. And one insecurity can often spread like a disease through your whole spirit. An actor's insecurities can cripple him, stop him from being able to do anything. Craft is the anti-dote. Having a craft will enable you to live with your insecurities and function not in spite of them but in terms of them. Insecurity is the feeling that you don't know how to do, or that you cannot do what is expected of you. BUT if you know what to do—and you know that you know—and you know HOW to do it, then you will do it and not be insecure about it.

The need to succeed and be good looms large as another cause of tension in actors. Once upon a time in Japan, a young man desirous of learning the art of the Samurai consulted with the oldest and greatest master of Samurai. He said, "Honorable Master, I wish to become the greatest Samurai in the world. I will study diligently. How long will it take me?" The Master replied, "Ten years." The student was shocked. "No, no, Honorable Master, you don't understand. I will live, eat, sleep and breathe the Samurai. I will think of nothing else! You see, I must be great. If I live, eat, sleep and breathe the Samurai and think of nothing else, *then* how long will it take me?" The Master's answer was, "In that case, twenty years."

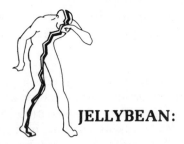

JELLYBEAN:

Sometimes Less Is More

Impatience and the need to succeed and be good are demons. It is quite natural that people want to succeed in what they do. Much of our personal and financial gain comes from a job well done. Even from childhood a certain competitiveness is instilled in us by our parents. People often come to the profession of acting out of a need for love and recognition and admiration. Their uppermost need is to be *good*. If an actor is mature enough to train his instrument and if he has talent and is willing to work for many years, trying and failing and trying some more, then he will be "good" *creatively* and he will achieve satisfaction in his art.

If, however, your need to be good is so strong that it prevents you from experimentation and squelches your courage to try things which might lead to failure, then you will cling to the things which you know you can do. By playing it safe your real talent will atrophy and your unique contribution will never be born. The great people of history in any field have been those with the courage to take chances, those who have investigated and questioned things, those who have made decisions in the face of any kind of opposition. You, the actor, are unique and individual, different from any other actor in the world. Your greatest contribution to the theatre will be what you can give of yourself to it. If you are willing to fail, and by failing, to learn, then you may discover the full dimensions of your talent. However, it is difficult to find this willingness in ourselves, because we are not allowed many failures as actors before producers become reluctant to hire us.

The actor *must* have a place to fail. There are workshops, classes, experimental theatres all over. These are the places where we can allow ourselves the NECESSITY of failing. The peculiar paradox is that when we are ready to accept failure as a necessary part of growth, we succeed more often than those who will not allow themselves to be bad. Tension is nurtured by the need to succeed and be good. If the need is so strong that the very thought of failure is unbearable, then quite a tension problem will result.

Among the most prevalent causes of tension are the absence of craft and the lack of faith in the instrument. Craft and faith are interrelated. Faith in your instrument comes from the security of having a concrete craft. It's quite possible to have a lot of faith without craft, and, conversely, a lot of craft without faith. Either way you're in trouble. It's true that faith alone may carry you a great distance, but faith based on accidental, hit-or-miss skill is not dependable. If you have craft, but no faith in it, then you can't use what you know.

The beginning actor is an interesting phenomenon. He has little or no training and often a great deal less tension than the experienced actor who has worked many years in the theatre. The beginner will often "jump in" courageously and commit himself totally. He hasn't discovered the complexities of creation. He knows very little of what is at stake and has a blind faith in his great intuitive talent. He or she is not "on the spot," because there isn't any spot yet! This explains why many actors feel they were better off before they began to study and, peculiarly, they may have been freer. But as their realization of what is expected grows, their freedom turns to terror unless they've been buiding a craft.

The ideal state is to believe that the craft you're learning and using is a workable approach to acting and that it will do for you, personally, what you want it to do. Your craft and your faith in it will come from trial-failure-success, work, work, work, work!

Another phenomenon related to tension is the actor who can't function *without it.* This is a very common and dangerous tension problem. This kind of actor works directly off his tension and cannot act unless he feels a great turmoil within. He's in fine shape on opening night when there is always a great deal of tension. He feels good on the first and second days of shooting a film because, in the midst of all the uncertainties, he's thrown on the spot in front of the camera and has to come through with a performance. But as he becomes more secure, his tension naturally becomes less and he has to stimulate it artificially in order to act. I call this acting problem "Theatrical Hysteria" or "Ass Energy." The actor's creative energy is really just nervous tension.

He doesn't recognize it as such and that's what makes Theatrical Hysteria so dangerous. Some actors have based entire careers on Ass Energy. You've seen them. The contorted faces, the clenched teeth, muscles stretched to the breaking point, the constant criers and sobbers. The actor himself is convinced that what he's feeling is great emotional experiences coming from deep within him. Without this sensation he feels naked. When his natural tension dissipates and he must artificially manufacture it, he thinks he's "preparing." What he is actually doing is giving himself a diarrhetic flow of tension, which passes for and takes the place of what he really feels. The tragedy is that he robs himself of genuine emotional experience.

THE "ACTRESS"

Recently in a private lesson I was working with a professional actress who is frequently seen on television. She was preparing a monologue from "Virginia Woolf." She started by pulling herself together, sitting upright in the chair, taking deep breaths, readying herself for what she knew was to come. She stared at an empty chair as if creating an imaginary person. Within seconds her eyes filled with tears. Her chest began to heave. The muscle at the side of her jaw pulsed in and out like a metronome. She exploded into a flow of words heavy with emotion. For five minutes she went on, standing up and beating the air with her fists. When she had finished, she sat down and again pulled herself together. Melodramatically, as if the experience had just been too much for her, she turned to me and I saw on her face a radiant self-satisfaction. She said, "Well? What do you think?"

I took several moments before I decided to tell her what I thought. It was obvious to me she'd been working this way for a long time and liking it. For my criticism to get through to her I'd really have to be honest with her. I decided that her process of work was infinitely more destructive to her than anything I could tell her.

She said, smiling, "Eric, I'm waiting."

I said, "I didn't believe one micro-second of what I saw. It was nonsense."

Her face fell. She was shocked. "What do you mean? How can you say that? I *felt* all those things!"

"I don't question that you felt something. But do you know why you and I are in conflict about the work? Why I think you're looking for ways to cut and run from here? Because I don't give you what you want. I don't tell you how talented and beautiful you are and how excited I am by your emotional outbursts when you do "Virginia Woolf" and "Dylan" and "Moony's Kid Don't Cry." I don't tell you that because it's all general neurotic emotion. Its origin is general. When you get on the stage to act, you magically and mystically fill up with all this conglomerated emotion, the tears, the rage, the retching. And you *think* this is the flow, the mainline flow, of your talent. But it's actually your tension, your fear of failure, your anxiety and your need for love and acceptance and your desire to be acclaimed as a creative artist, rolled up into a ball of theatrically hysterical emotion. You pay lip service to working for a choice, but actually you take that conglomerated, neurotic emotion and box it into "Virginia Woolf" or wrap it into "Dylan." It's fraudulent, impure. You've been "passing" for a finely tuned emotional instrument, but in reality you're a fraud. You're short-changing yourself ninety-eight cents out of every talent dollar you possess. No, I'm not going to give you what you want. I want to give you what you need. And you need to let go of what you depend on and run the risk of getting *nothing,* until that nothing becomes reality."

DEALING WITH TENSION

We have now discussed some of the major causes of tension, though certainly not all of them. You'll find the rest of this chapter rich in remedies. At the risk of being redundant, we stress the importance of recognizing your tension, acknowledging it and then proceeding systematically to alleviate it. As soon as you ask a question, you will begin getting answers. Where am I tense? Where in my body do I feel discomfort? Where is it moving to now? It's logical that the more questions you ask the more answers you get.

Each person has different tension points. Usually the tension will find its way to the same points and once you become aware of these places you'll find it easier to help yourself. Pinpoint the areas, admit them and encourage the tension to express itself. "I feel tight in my shoulders. Hello, tension in the shoulders. I know you're there. My knees are shaking. Okay, knees. Shake." If you find your hands are trembling, encourage them to do that. Let it show. When you find all your shaking and trembling and tightness has reached a peak, then simply ask those parts of your body to relax. Let your hands hang loosely and be pulled naturally by gravity.

Your tension points are the areas that the tension finds in hopes of getting out. It must be released somehow. If there is a denial of its presence and it is stifled at every outlet, it will bounce around inside and totally cut the actor off from either being affected by a stimulus or having an honest response to one. The actor who shows his tension is better off than the one who has it under control, because when it's closer to the surface it can be spotted and dealt with. Identify the tension in all parts of your body in the same way—face, chest, stomach, pelvis, legs, feet, etc.

There are thousands of ways to deal with tension problems. Try anything that you feel might do the job. At times one thing will work

40

and at other times the very thing that worked before will fail. It's wise to know and to have tried many techniques. Knowing what to use depends largely on knowing yourself, knowing what things affect you, and when.

Besides identifying and acknowledging your tension, you will find you can also help yourself by getting *involved*. Tension is usually the result of being concerned with yourself. It follows that if you can transfer that concern away from yourself, you'll get rid of your self-consciousness. Ask yourself simple questions such as: "How many colors can I count on this stage?" Count them. "How many set pieces do I see here?" Count them. Relate to the objects around you by asking personal questions about them such as, "What does that couch mean to me? Have I ever seen one like it? In whose house?" Often the answers to your questions will kick off a certain behavioral relationship to these objects. Ask a question about the people you're working with. "What are the most attractive features about that girl? Who does she remind me of? Is there any resemblance between her and any other woman I know? If so, what features are alike and what features are different?" And on and on. If you allow the responses that have been stimulated by these questions to express themselves, you will begin to function quite organically and creatively.

Sometimes the tension will be stuffed down inside you, compacted into many layers. It may be impossible to connect with it in any of the ways we've mentioned. It will be necessary to do a more active and drastic preparation. Here you'll find useful the Abandonment group of exercises.

When your ego is involved and affecting your state of tension, then choose any of the exercises in the Ego group. In the meantime, you might take yourself off the spot by asking yourself questions such as: "Is it possible for me to please everybody? Of course not. So why try? Can I do anything about the way people think? Not really. Who must I ultimately please?" You know the answer to that one and you'll discover that you are the one who expects the most from you. Why not just begin with the goal of pleasing yourself, and if you get close to doing that, you will please many people along with yourself.

As you become more involved in a specific craft, a creative approach to your work will emerge and some of your reasons for acting may undergo a change. You might find that your relationship to acting is now on a deeper level than what originally attracted you to the art. You might find that in the excitement of creation lies the real

41

fulfillment of your needs. Your acting will then acquire a more courageous attack. You will be achieving tasks that you've set for yourself rather than working for praise, acceptance and recognition. As the obligation to succeed diminishes, so will the tension caused by it.

The actor should have a group of exercises that work for him or her, depending on the situation and personal need. In my classes I like to start with physical relaxation exercises such as Logey, Rag Doll, Tense and Relax. But other exercises, which we'll talk about here, relieve physical tension as a result of getting involved in something other than yourself, or as a result of large expurgative actions. The actor learns what's most effective for him and collects his own tools.

JELLYBEAN:

In Order To Act You Must Be Relaxed. In Order To Relax You Must Help Yourself To Relax. In Order To Be, You Must Include Everything You Are. It Takes Courage.

THE PHYSICAL RELAXERS

The exercises in this category deal primarily with the existence of physical tension, although many of the exercises in every category may serve more than one purpose.

1. Tense and Relax

Lie down on the floor, or remain standing if necessary. Starting from your feet, tighten slowly by degrees each part of your body, holding it tight until your whole body is rigid. Then from the top of your head start relaxing by degrees slowly, until you return to where you started. Do this two or three times. The exercise forces your muscles to relax by tiring them and it also teaches your body to recognize the varying degrees of tension so that when you experience tension on stage, you'll be more specifically aware of it and able to deal with it. It's essential to learn how to do this for yourself, because it takes a lot of muscular tension to keep impulses suppressed, and when this muscular tension is relieved, the impulses flow.

2. Logey

Logey is one of my invented words and to me it means heavy, slothful and lethargic. This is the physical state and feeling you want to achieve. Lie down on the floor, flat on your back at first. Later you'll find your own Logey positions. Become aware of the weight of your body, the weight of your head, of your limbs, of your thorax, your pelvis, thighs, legs. People support their weight through muscular tension and energy so that we never think that the head weighs fifteen pounds or more, but if we release that support, that head feels heavy. Start the exercise, becoming aware of your normal weight. Then increase and expand the sense of your weight until you feel even heavier. Test your Logey by lifting your arms one at a time and letting them fall of their own weight. Do this with all parts of the body, feeling the pull of gravity on each part. By removing the body's support, you remove its physical tension.

3. Rag Doll

Stand up on both feet and from the top of your head, let yourself be pulled toward the ground, one vertebra at a time, until you finally crumple on the floor in a rag heap. Do it slowly, letting your arms hang loosely at your sides. When you reach the knees, bend them.

4. Original *BEING*

This exercise requires more time—about an hour—and it does more than just relax you. It sensitizes you and makes you keenly aware of things around you that you've never noticed. Do it either sitting up or lying down, preferably lying down. Clear your mind of thoughts and try to achieve a kind of wakeful sleep. Then slowly awaken, as if for the first time. You are fully grown with your normal intelligence and musculature, but no prior experience of anything at all. You see, hear, feel, taste, smell everything as if for the first time. You have your own muscular abilities, but without the knowledge of how even to move your hand.

All of this must be discovered and learned. Original BEING can be used for other purposes besides relaxation. It's an anti-intellectual, anti-premeditative process. After you do it, you realize how many things you take for granted and how often you premeditate your responses to things and to people.

5. Deep Breathing

Lie down and breathe more deeply with each breath you take. Exhale as fully as you inhale. Breathe as if your body were a hollow vessel and all the air you breathe will finally reach down to the soles of your feet.

6. Abandonment

This exercise is useful when you're enormously tense and you have to blast through your barricades. It is large, physically and vocally. Clear a good space for yourself in the room. Remove necklaces, glasses, watches and any object that could hurt you. Do it on a carpet or a fairly soft ground surface. With *abandonment,* hurl yourself into what might resemble having a physical "fit," kicking, flailing your body in every direction, screaming, howling and being as vocally abandoned as you are physically. The exercise should go on until you're spent. When it's over, you might cry or laugh or experience a large emotional expurgation of some kind. This exercise, besides getting rid of your tension, can also be used to get down deeper and free reluctant emotions.

7. Dump

This is based on Dr. George Bach's Vesuvius exercise, and like the Abandonment, it's also a large expurgative. Start expressing all your frustrations, dissatisfactions, angers, disappointments, needs, desires until you achieve an eruptive flow of all that has been suppressed. You are then free to move past it and go on to other things.

8. Dealing with the Demon

I found out something about tension in working with actors in the classroom and in commercial situations. Once you identify tension, verbally acknowledge its presence in you and what it's doing to you at that moment, the tension moves around. It's elusive. You might feel it in your chest, identify it and then it jumps down to your legs. It finds another hiding place. I invented this exercise to train actors to hunt the demon—and it is a demon—tension is the original demon—and to expose it. For instance, the actor might be feeling a kind of general relaxation, but when he starts to speak, his voice quivers. The tension has gone into his voice-box. I acted in a film recently and before the take, I'd done preparations, felt relaxed and related to the actress working with me, ready to do the scene. Then they called "Action" and two lines later, the demon put his hand on the back of my neck and my whole head started to shake.

The enemy to tension is exposure. If you allow it to stay hidden, it compounds itself. But if you expose it publicly, out loud, you no longer have the need to be better off that you really are. *Everybody knows you're tense and instead of the charade, you can get down to the business of ridding yourself of it.*

This exercise is also done in a stream-of-consciousness fashion, as many of the exercises are, in order to stimulate a moment-to-moment flow of reality. Verbally—out loud or semi-audibly—and preferably in front of the people you're working with, chase your demon as it scurries through your body. For example: "Oh, I feel tension in the back of my neck. Hello there, Demon. Oh, it just moved down to my shoulder. It's in my right shoulder. That's funny, I just became aware that my stomach is a little jumpy. It's down there now. It's both in my shoulders and my stomach now. I'm looking around, seeing everybody working on the set. Who's that person the director's talking to? Oh, oh, I just felt it insidiously creeping into my back. Hello, Demon. I know where you are. My throat is closing up a little bit. I'm taking a deep breath and it's okay. I know you're there. I know all the places where you are and

I'm going to allow you to be there, because I can't deny you . . . " and so forth, until you feel ready to work.

Joan uses the following variation of Dealing with the Demon, which is based on a Gestalt exercise. "I locate the Demon outside of myself. I place it on a chair or on some object across from me and then I talk to it as Joan. I say things like, 'I'm sick and tired of you, Black Fear. You've plagued me all my life. You turn my bowels to water and make my throat dry and take all the fun out of acting. I exhaust myself trying to get rid of you, but you always come back.' And then I switch roles and become the Demon talking to Joan. I'll say something like, 'Oh, come off it, Joan, you're kidding yourself trying to be an actress. You're middle-aged and you haven't made it and you'll never make it. You missed your calling. You really should have been somebody's fat wife in the suburbs.' And then I'll be Joan again and talk back to it. 'Stop that! You get away from me! I'm doing what I love to do and you're not going to drag me down!' I'll spend sometimes as long as a half hour on this dialogue and by the end of it I feel freer, more centered in my self-esteem, less victimized by a vague enemy and the reason is because I've made that enemy very specific. The dialogue exposes to me the kind of negative self-talk that I inflict upon my faith. It objectifies my Demon."

 **JELLYBEAN:**

If I Am Not For Me, Then Who Will Be?

9. Expose Innermost Feelings in Gibberish

Sometimes we get tense not because we're on the spot, but because we have a mountain of unexpressed feelings and impulses that we have not vented. A lot of these things might be so private or personal that to vent them in words might have undesirable consequences. You need to express these pent-up feelings so that you can get beneath and beyond them to other kinds of life. You can express them in gibberish, releasing your impulses without violating your privacy. This exercise is most effective, as many of these exercises are, when done in front of other people.

10. The Ingestion Exercise

I devised this exercise in a private lesson with an actor and then later found it valuable for many actors. It is non-verbal, but very vocal. With gesture and sound, you take into your body and ingest all the objects around you, growing larger and louder and stronger and more powerful with each ingestion, until you feel you're a giant ball of energy and power. This exercise is exciting to watch when done well because in a minute you see a human being grow in stature and become enormously compelling on stage.

THE INVOLVEMENT GROUP

The exercises so far have related to dealing with the self, which requires self-involvement. But often tension can be relieved by getting involved in something outside of yourself. The following exercises fall into this category.

11. Taking Responsibility for Others

Taking Responsibility for Others is designed to get you off the spot by involving you with things outside of yourself. Do it standing up, using the people around you, your rehearsal group or classroom. Express what you observe about these people as selflessly as possible, excluding the word "I" as much as you can and also excluding any personal relations you might have with them. Try objectively to help each person be better off than he is right now, giving specifically constructive suggestions. The word "responsibility" is the key to this exercise. If you really feel responsible for helping the other person, then something immediately becomes more important to you than you and your tension.

12. Total Selflessness

This is similar to the one above except that you don't take responsibility for helping anyone. You relate to your environment, observing it and commenting on it without ever using the pronoun "I" or relating anything back to yourself. For example, "That's a beautiful bush. It smells marvelous. You really seem to be creatively involved in what you're doing. This place has a fantastic view, doesn't it? You don't seem to take advantage of the beauty around you . . ." And so forth. Just because you're excluding the word "I" does not mean that you are not affected by the things you're observing. The exercise usually succeeds in getting you out of yourself.

13. The Trivial Trio

Say the Alphabet Backwards

Count Your Own Heartbeats

Say a Line of Dialogue Backwards

These exercises are simple devices for placing your energy in an area away from your concerns with self.

14. Threshold of Interest

This exercise is non-verbal. Look around you and investigate the things that interest you with all five senses, going from object to object only as you are impelled to. This encourages you to get involved in things outside of yourself without obligations.

INTERNAL AWARENESS

An actor's preparation must include a working process to increase his awareness, his awareness of what's going on inside him and what's happening in the world around him. The more things you're aware of, the more things you're affected by. The more things you're affected by, the more kinds of emotional life you experience, and, therefore, the more levels of life you have to draw from in creating the behavior of different kinds of people.

At any given moment, billions of things are happening both inside and out. Naturally you can't be aware of even a fraction of all that—the sound all the way down to the sounds of silence, the smells, the colors and shapes around you and the infinite spectrum of your inner feelings about all these things, your personal point of view. But if you keep stretching your awareness, you'll have a larger and larger living canvas. Stimulus, effect, response and expression— this is the natural order. The greater the number of things that you're aware of and available to, the richer your talent.

All of the following exercises in the Internal Awareness Group are explained in detail in Chapter I. As has been said before, many of these exercises are multi-purposed.

15. Personal Inventory I

16. Personal Inventory II

17. What Do I Want?

18. I Am, I Want, I Need, I Feel

EXTERNAL AWARENESS

Since a large part of eliminating tension is based on involvement away from the problem, becoming aware and related to things around you is a natural progression. This group of exercises relates to objects, places and people outside of yourself.

19. Nature Walk

This is a rich investigation of your environment. Take a walk outdoors, ideally in a place where nature is overwhelming—the mountains, the sea, the snows. But your own backyard is fine too. Become aware of everything around you on every sensory level—smell, taste, touch, sight, sound. Pick up a leaf and study the vein structure. Smell it. Crush it in your fingers and feel the texture. Taste it. Lose yourself in the life of that leaf. Then broaden your awareness to include the fullness of the whole tree, the distance between the tree and the mountain, the shadows from the sunlight, the sun on your face, the way the ground feels under your feet as you walk. Explore everything you can and allow yourself to be affected emotionally. You may be affected in many different ways. You might be overwhelmed by the smallness of your size in relation to the universe or elated by the fragrances.

20. Awareness Levels

This is a running verbal account of all the levels of your sensory awareness as they happen. It encourages your gradual and increasing awareness of the subtleties and complexities of the immediate environment. Don't evaluate, analyze or comment on how you feel about any of it. "That dog barking is terribly loud. A plane overhead, faint. Now I hear the motorcycle. Bird just flew out from under the eaves. Bird twittering. Door slammed in the house. Odor of the flowered bush and now it went away. Cool breeze across my left knee. Plane very faint overhead. Breeze moving the bushes. Noticed the pattern of the bricks in the patio. Some kind of fumble coming from somewhere. Fingerpads sore from typing." As you do this exercise, you'll become more aware of increasing subtleties in your awareness, levels beneath the levels.

21.   Observe, Wonder and Perceive I

Like Personal Inventory, this is a craft-backbone exercise and has many purposes. For now we'll confine ourselves to what it can do for your awareness. You can do it silently, semi-audibly or audibly with people. Start simply by observing the things you observe and express that. "I observe that you look tired." Then you might add, "I wonder, are you tired? Are you not feeling well? I perceive from your behavior that you don't want to answer that question. You look angry. I wonder if you're angry. I wonder, do you color your hair? You look like you've been working hard." The exercise is a monologue. It doesn't have to relate to people and it isn't necessary to preface each wonderment or perception with "I wonder" or "I perceive." But use these phrases at first to keep from slipping back into self-involvement.

22.   Farmer's Market

I call this the Farmer's Market Exercise because I used to take my class there every Wednesday morning to learn to observe human behavior. The Farmer's Market is loaded with people of all nationalities and from all parts of our country. It's a bountiful place in which to do this exercise, but you can do the exercise anywhere—in a restaurant, a park, a museum, on a bus or subway or in the lobby of a movie house.

Getting ready to get ready is a living process, a daily process, and a vitally important part of it is to observe how people behave when they are BEING. Most actors learn to act from watching other actors act on television and in films and so they become imitative of bad acting habits. BEING is a foreign state to them. Watching an actor on stage in a workshop scene and then observing him afterwards listening to the criticism—the difference is incredible. When he's listening and responding, just BEING, he is filled with emotional colors and contrasts and unpredictable fleeting thoughts that cross his face. We don't know what he's going to do, because he doesn't. His life has all the dimensions of reality.

There are many reasons for practicing observation exercises. It trains you to get involved more objectively in things outside of yourself instead of being limited by your own subjective concerns. It stretches your perception, which increases your affectability; the more you perceive, the more you respond to. As you develop skill in observation, you will learn to isolate elements of human behavior and define their origins so that later, on stage, you can create stimuli that will produce similar behavior in you. This exercise can be used as a means of getting an external sense of another person as a tool for characterization. It's important for you to observe and understand all kinds of human behavior and idiosyncrasies, because you have to deal with all levels and facets of behavior in your work.

There are specific things you look for when you are observing people. These are the categories of observation:

a)   **How Is the Person Dressed?**
How he's dressed has a lot to do with what that person's all about. The style, the apparent cost of the clothes, comfort or discomfort, color coordination, the concern or lack of concern with his own clothing, whether it's in or out of style, etc. The person may be a millionaire wearing blue jeans that day. You take that chance. Fortunately, it isn't the only thing you see and you cross-reference with other observations.

b)   **Props**
What do people have protruding from their pockets? What is he holding onto? What is she carrying? What is he wearing in addition to the clothing-jewelry, a hat, pipe, cigarette holder. A man who has a plastic-lined pocket in his shirt filled with six pencils obviously does something with pencils. He has that liner to protect his shirt. Now if he's wearing a suit, he does something with pencils that work clothes don't go with. Possibly some kind of clerical position. A person with a briefcase might be moving around from place to place. The books people carry tell you a lot about their taste in literature or about their work. Also observe the way people relate to their "props." Are they careful with them? Or careless? How do they open their car doors? Are they worried about the paint?

c)   **Involvements and Relationships**
Suppose a person is totally involved in what he's doing to the exclusion of everything around him. Is he doing this protec-

tively to keep from having to deal with other people and things around him? Or is he more interested in what he's doing than in his environment? Or is he so involved with himself that he's unaware of the surroundings? Or is he under pressure of some kind? Is he late? What are the specifics that suggest a person's involvement? You might be able to tell whether a man is out to lunch with his secretary by the way he relates to her. Is he coming on to her sexually or are they just talking business? Is he concerned with being seen by anybody? Is he married or not? You can tell if people have been intimate with each other by the way they relate. You can almost tell at what point in a relationship two people are by observing how they relate to each other. Are they at the beginning of a romantic relationship or at the end? You can almost guess how many times they've been intimate with each other. You may be wrong, but that's okay. Keep on observing and deducing.

d) **Awareness or the Lack of It**
How does the person relate to his own body? How aware is he of his own physicality? How unaware? A person who is a physical culturist, a weight-lifter, relates to his body in a way that calls attention to it. A woman who reached pubescence too soon and hated her large breasts may still be hunched over, trying to hide them.

How do people relate to the weather? Do they seem aware of what kind of day it is? Are they aware of the other people around them? Of the place? Some people function no further than six inches away from their faces and don't get involved with things that demand a response.

e) **Compensations and Redirections**
Compensation is a behavior which is superimposed over what you really feel. It's a subtle thing that clings to a person like a behavioral veil. For example, a lady customer at a counter is given the wrong change and politely accepts it and walks away. Or she quietly asks for the correct change, please, and the salesperson yells, "Will you wait a minute, I only got two hands!" The customer smiles and says pleasantly, "All right." That's compensation. You know she's not feeling all right at all. She's feeling something else. Or another example, someone walks into a party and is tense and self-conscious, but compensates for it by being limp-wristed and "super-relaxed."

Many characters in plays behave compensationally. These observations help you to understand the complexity of these behaviors and later to create them.

Redirection is feeling one thing and putting it into another more socially acceptable. For instance, someone who feels like crying might laugh instead, because the thought of shedding a tear is shameful. You can tell that the laughter is not pure. It's redirection and belies the reality. If you train yourself to observe, you'll see the underlying truths.

f) **Self-Consciousness**
The quickest way to spot people's sensitivities, the things they're anxious about, is to watch how they point to it like beacons in the night. The short guy accentuates his shortness by standing up to his full height so that he calls attention to his size. The very tall, lanky guy who slumps also calls attention to his own concern about his height. People who are embarrassed about their teeth often talk behind their hand or keep the top lip stiff so you can't see their teeth. A woman who had teen-age acne and now has a face that is pocked with scars never moves her face at all as she talks to you. The immobility, which she believes is concealing, only rivets your eyes to her face. You, the observer, can become expert in identifying self-consciousness and the various ways people attempt to handle it.

g) **Eating and Other Activities**
How someone relates to food reveals to you whether eating is a big moment in his day or not. Some people eat as if it were the entire consummation of life. You can observe someone eating lunch as if he had prepared for this moment yesterday. Another might always leave something on her plate because a Southern *lady* never cleans her plate. You can tell if someone had a weight problem by the way he relates to food even though he's not fat. It's all deductive observation which is seeing how people do what they do and then deducing the reasons for it. To keep from falling into the trap of script-writing, continually ask yourself, "What tells me that?"

h) **Time-Capsule**
This observation can spread over all the categories. The way a person dresses, eats, relates to things around him might be walking out of a 1947 calendar or a 1950 movie magazine.

This was probably the most exciting time of life for him and nothing that followed equaled it. This is the point where his curiosity died and the striving to grow ended. Look for evidence of this in hair and clothing style, colloquialisms, slang of another era, sexual morality and nostalgic stories.

Your deductions might seem outrageously unfounded. But encourage yourself to wonder, ask, imagine and conclude. Take chances. If you're wrong, fine. You're strengthening your curiosity and adventurousness on and off the stage so that in searching for a character in a play, you'll be more likely to come up with fresh, unconventional but entirely human discoveries.

PURPOSES OF THE FARMER'S MARKET EXERCISE

- To increase your perception of behavior, its origins, its variety and peculiarities.

- To make you aware of where, how and why people behave.

- To increase your affectability.

- To give you a barometer of your own behavior in terms of its authenticity, because you have a life model.

- To help you understand and create behavior that isn't your own, to help you get a sense of other people.

What are realities? How do you create realities? You create the source, not the manifestation.

Do it every day.

SENSORY AWARENESS

Discovering your senses and how they work is an essential aspect of getting ready to get ready. We will go deeply into sense memory, but for now, let's start with discovering the senses. Your five senses are your doors of perception. Through these doors comes everything that has ever affected you and you are the sum total of all these things. Knowing how each of your senses works, individually and personally, opens your doors wider and teaches you to use your senses in a creative process.

Your five senses are:

1.   **Visual**
      Everything you see. Seeing.

2.   **Tactile**
      Feeling, touching, everything that comes into contact with your skin.

3.   **Auditory**
      Hearing.

4.   **Olfactory**
      Smelling.

5.   **Gustatory**
      Tasting.

5½.   **Kinesthetic**
      A muscular response to real and imaginary objects. It's part of the tactile area, but it's deeper than just an epidermal response. Blind people develop this part of their sensory equipment much more fully than people who see. In class I discovered the importance of the fifth-and-a-half sense by putting two actors with their backs to each other about six inches apart and told them to communicate without touch, sound or sight. I found out that people could feel not only the presence of another person, but also that person's physical and emotional attitude. It's elusive, but it can be perceived. Sitting in a movie theatre you feel the presence of someone behind you and when that person leaves you feel the absence. It's your kinesthetic response to something there that was not there before or is not there now.

23. Sensory Inventory: How the Senses Work

Long before I ever thought of teaching acting I studied with someone who introduced me to sense memory and I began an intense exploration of it on my own. I worked with my senses for hours every day. I really had to find out how my senses functioned, why they would respond to a certain thing. How do I know that cold is cold and not hot, or blue? What tells me that?

I became quite a fanatic about it because my search was so exciting and engrossing. The phenomenal thing about sense memory is when it starts to work for you, when you start to feel, *really* feel the heat of an imaginary flame, when you start to sweat in a cold room or get gooseflesh in a hot room. You feel unique, elite, one of the chosen few.

First of all, I isolated each sense and concentrated on one at a time. I'd try to find out where on my hand I felt anything and why I felt more in some parts of my hand than in others. I'd take the end of a pencil and run it slowly down the inside of my hand from the tip of my fingers to my wrist and I'd find that at the very tip of my finger, just below the fingernail, I didn't feel as much as on the pad of my finger. I concluded that there must be more nerve endings in the pad than on the tip. I also discovered that the finger pads are more sensitive than the second joint of each finger. I'd take a matchbook or coffee cup or whatever object I was working with and explore the insides of my fingers with it, moving it to the back of my hand, touching it to my cheek, up the arm and all over the rest of my body. I found out many things, such as that the parts of me usually covered with clothing were more sensitive to temperature and texture than the exposed parts. Holding an ice cube in each hand, I'd explore how long it took for the cold to numb my sense. I'd take off my shoes and walk around barefoot feeling the differences between the rug and the tile floor and I'd attempt to relate to objects with my feet as I usually did with my hands, picking things up off the floor.

Then I might go to my nose and investigate my sense of smell. I'd fill a tabletop with a variety of odors—a perfume, a chocolate bar, a lemon, sachets, can of coffee. I found that by sniffing deeper, throwing the odors back into my nose the way a dog does, I smelled more fully and more kinds of odors. I decided that an odor must be the molecules of the object floating up into the air and getting up into the nose to be interpreted by the brain. I'd ask myself questions. Where is smell taking place in my nose? Where exactly do I smell? Which nostril do I get the most response from? I'd cover one nostril and then the other. I realized that the olfactory sense gets saturated very quickly. There'd come a point where I couldn't smell any of the objects on the table and I'd have to walk away for a while. Then I'd come back and try to define the specific parts of each odor and exactly where in my nose I smelled it.

In tasting, I found that I taste with the roof of my mouth as well as the sides, the top and the tip of my tongue and in the cheeks. I've talked to people who've gotten dentures which cover up the roof of the mouth and they tell me they lose a portion of their taste and have to learn to compensate with the other parts of their mouth.

I found that in my mouth I taste a great deal on the sides of my tongue so that in rolling things around, such as a piece of hard candy, I'd experience bursts of flavor when it got to certain parts of my mouth. Then I'd try it with coffee with cream and sugar in it. I'd roll the coffee around and when I'd get to the same section, the sides of my tongue and under my tongue, there'd be bursts of flavor. I'd suck in air while I had liquid in my mouth, as wine-tasters do, and the air, mixed with the liquid, for some reason enhanced the taste. Maybe the air excited the receptors, the taste buds. I think I even taste with my gums. I'm not sure of that, but I know my teeth *feel*. You can take a pencil and put it between your top and bottom teeth and you can feel textures and shapes. For years that's how people found out if a pearl was real or fake. The real pearl has little irregular bumps on it that are perceived by the teeth. Of course, with any object in my mouth I'd always be aware of temperature and texture even though I was concentrating on the sense of taste and not the tactile sense.

Visually, my eyes were attracted to what interested them at first— colors, shapes, sizes. The eye skips over many details of an object. The visual sense has a tendency to take a lot for granted and unless we train it to be specific, it just takes in the overall object. When I'd focus on something and then look away, I'd experience an after-image like the negative of a photo. I worked with each eye individually and found differences and peculiarities of each one. I explored dimension by holding up my finger in front of my face and quickly blinking one eye and then the other. I'd look at the texture of an object and then touch it and check out the difference between what my eyes told me the texture was and what my tactile sense told me. My eyes investigated the depth of objects and the distances between them. I'd blind myself momentarily with a bright light, and then find out how long it took for my sight to return.

I really enjoyed playing with my ears. Ears are shaped conically to trap sound. People whose ears stick out from the head hear better, so I'd point my ear in certain directions and cup it with my hand and, like a radar cone, I'd hear more of the subtleties. You get close to finding out how you sound to other people by cupping your ears and talking. I'd turn a piece of music on very loud and then very low and move my head in various directions trying to find out at what point I was the most sensitive. I tried to break down sounds into vibrations to learn how I hear and to find out what hearing is. Sounds that come directly in front of you or in back of you are hard to determine in terms of their direction, their origin. I'd plug up both ears just to listen to the sounds of my own body and I discovered that my own body is very noisy. I could hear the coursing of my blood, the pounding of my heart, swallowing, breathing and digesting.

Finding out how your senses work is an exciting adventure. You will become your own pathfinder and the paths are infinite. The more you explore your sensory apparatus, the more totally you will be able to use it in the craft of acting.

24. Sensitizing

This exercise should be done daily. We do it at the beginning of each class, because it's an essential element of the actor's preparation. It enormously heightens your sensory availability.

It can be done in any position. As in the Sensory Inventory, the exercise requires the isolation of the senses. Start with the tactile sense, beginning with the top of your head, your scalp. It's as if you are *living* in your scalp. When your scalp begins to tingle or you feel a pulse there or the heat of your own body, it's an indication that that part is sensitized. Then you move to your forehead, your face, your chin. Move down your body in four-inch sections until you get to the soles of your feet, living in each section until you feel it is sensitized.

Then go to your ears. Without touching them with your hands, become aware of their structure. Then, as you did in the tactile area, *live* in your ears. Listen to every sound from the most obvious to the most subtle, their directions and origins, all the way down to the component parts of silence.

Then the nose. Become aware of its structure without touching it, the apertures, the mucous membrane, the inner nose. Live in your nose. Become aware of all the odors around you. Try to smell all of them and the elements of each one. It's as if you've become a giant nose.

Then to the mouth. Focus on it, the gums, the teeth, tongue, cheeks. Taste the tastes in your own mouth. You might have some toothpaste left over from brushing your teeth. You might have a coffee taste or the aftertaste of a sandwich. Do it until you taste even the taste of your own flesh.

You can sensitize your eyes in one of two ways. Isolate a small area, maybe the corner of a table top, and, by living in your eyes, attempt to see every minute detail. Or look at an object, a small portion of it, and then look away and try to visualize that same portion. Then look back and go to another portion and repeat the same process, living in your eyes.

The entire exercise might take you fifteen minutes, or twenty, when you first do it, but as you practice it over a period of time, you condition your senses to respond instantly and you can do it all in less than two minutes.

GETTING TO THE DEEPER SELF

After becoming aware of how you feel and what's around you, it's important to reach down more deeply into yourself and begin finding a fuller relationship to who you are, what you feel, what you want, what you experience. You are as individual as your fingerprints and the unique contribution of that individuality is dependent on your getting to know all that is there and using it in your work. The following exercises are designed to help you get to your deeper self.

25. Stream of Consciousness

This is the verbalization of everything that you're thinking and feeling without the emphasis, as in Personal Inventory, on finding out how you feel. It establishes a moment-to-moment flow of everything that is going on. Doing this exercise regularly enables you to express everything without obstruction and frees all the impulses that go on underneath the level of life on which we usually live. It's an antidote to the habit of functioning above your real self.

26. I'm Afraid That . . .

A verbal stream in which each sentence begins with "I'm afraid that . . . " For example, "I'm afraid my agent is no good and I'll never work again. I'm afraid I'll get old and die alone. I'm afraid I won't succeed on the level I want, won't get recognition for what I know I am. I'm afraid of being poor. I'm afraid to go to that party tonight, all those people I don't know. I'm afraid to be afraid. I'm afraid people will know I'm afraid. I'm afraid my kid will grow up and be a bum. I'm afraid of falling in love." And on and on and on.

The value of this exercise is to put you in touch with your fears which you often hide from yourself. By exposing the fears, they become less crippling. And getting to know and express your fears is another step in the process of knowing yourself.

27.   I Like That . . .

The positive twin to "I'm Afraid That. . . ." "I like that I'm alive today. I like that I'm brushing my dog's fur. I like having breakfast in bed. I like that I worked out at the gym today. I'm excited about going out tonight. . . ." Here also you'll surprise yourself sometimes and find out likes you didn't know you had. It's also a good exercise for picking up your spirits.

28.   I Care, I Don't Care

Another type of verbal stream, emphasizing what you care about and what you don't care about. Express your caring and non-caring about everything from worldly issues to the most trivial objects around you.

29.   Personal Point of View

There are two ways to do this exercise—either to yourself and for yourself, or out loud in front of other people. Both ways help you to find out what your personal point of view is about anything; something you may not have known you had a point of view about at all. Saying it in front of others develops your courage to expose and take responsibility for what you feel.

30.   Center Circle

Any of these exercises can be done standing in the center of a circle of people and when done this way, each exercise takes on the added dimension of being on the spot.

Center Circle is also an exercise unto itself, the forerunner of Dealing with the Demon. In the center of the circle, you become aware of what being on the spot does to you, physically and emotionally. In verbally acknowledging that, you learn more about what affects you in that situation and how. The expression of how you feel frees you to function more comfortably.

31.   Personal Inventory

This exercise, already described in Chapter I, is an extremely important one in getting to the self. Add the question, "What do I want?" to "How do I feel?"

32. Self Inventory

Joan: Eric, is Self Inventory anything like Personal Inventory?

Eric: No, no, not at all. Self Inventory is a process of taking stock of your life—your day, the last month, the last year, five years ago, and so on. It's a recalling of emotional events in your life and other kinds of experiences, but most important, it's the cataloguing of the *sensory elements* of those experiences so that when you need those feelings later on in your work, you know the buttons to push. You've got the means to restimulate yourself.

Joan: I think I know what you mean. I do that a lot, mostly when I go to bed at night.

Eric: Yes, that's when I do it too. Actually it started when I was a boy and I used to hate to go to bed at night. I used to have to con myself into going to sleep. So I'd get in bed and make up stories, aggrandize myself, fantasize occurrences, be a famous actor with people applauding me. This is how I started to act, really. Then later on, in later years, when I was studying acting and having difficulty laying my hands on choices, I would go to bed at night and I would start to go over my day. What happened today? What was significant? Who did I see? I'd reconstruct the day sensorily, so to speak, without doing a sense memory exercise.

I went over the current day every night for about a month. Then for the next month or two I went back a week and picked a day out of that week and reconstructed it. After I could do that, I went back a whole month. And then I'd go back five or six months at random. I'd let my mind wander and say, "Okay, think of an experience, an important experience related to an important day . . . Okay, my birthday, November 19th . . . Okay, now I'm at November 19th . . . Did anything happen toward the beginning of the month? Yeah, I can remember something . . . Okay, what about something *after* my birthday, something toward the end of the month?" In other words, I'd use my birthday or any meaningful day as a center point from which to

61

work backwards and forwards. As I did Self Inventory, I found I could recall more and more going all the way back to the age of four and five and really remember smelling and tasting and hearing and feeling things. And I could really use all those things now. They were usable to me as an actor.

Joan: That's fabulous. But you know most people have difficulty remembering.

Eric: Oh, sure. Particularly after five years. It's vague and general.

Joan: That's right. People say to me, "Joan, how do you remember all that? That happened so long ago!"

Eric: Well, everything that's ever happened to us is locked in some brain cell, stored in the unconscious. We don't ever forget anything.

Joan: I found that out in psychoanalysis. One of the things analysis did for me, not to mention all of the things it didn't do for me, was it opened up my memory. I re-experienced very early events in my life and these events are purely sensory, Eric, because that's before you know any words.

Eric: I never could remember my childhood. I mean really, not past a certain point. I couldn't remember below ten except fragmentary images—my father walking through the door lifting me up—my mother dressing me for school. But they were fleeting images. Until I started doing Self Inventory and stretched my memory. I made up the exercise to help myself as an actor and then later when I began teaching, I discovered a lot of actors need it.

Joan: You said you kept a journal too.

Eric: Yes, I did, for a while. And that's another way you can do Self Inventory. There are two ways, really. The way I described, going back a day or a month or a year, and so on. And you can also keep a daily journal, writing down significant experiences of that day. You record not only the events, but also the sensory stimuli so that a year or two or three years from now you can look back in your journal to May 14th or May 15th and you have right there the whole experience—how you felt and all the sensory elements that made you feel that way.

Joan: I've kept a journal from time to time, but when I first started studying with you, you told me not to write anything down.

Eric: Because you were writing things down instead of learning them organically, but now you've grown beyond that. It's always a danger when actors put things in writing because they tend to feel it's been accomplished. They think they've done the work on it. But actually they haven't done the work on it. It's just the raw material.

Joan: I really understand that now. Listen, Eric, there's something I want to ask you. You know that romantic idealism we're looking for in the Swan Lake section of my play? I've been searching in various areas of my life and I think I've found something. It's the three summers I spent at Four Winds Camp when I was in my early teens. They were idyllic summers. See, look at this list here. These are the sensory fragments—my middy uniform, it was always starched and it had a certain smell to it. The various cabins that I stayed in. The balcony of the lodge at night and the feeling of girls' arms around my waist when we used to sing a goodnight song to each other. Roman Meal cereal, that crunchy texture. And the smells of pine and balsam and doughnuts frying.

Eric: These are all things you remembered from that time?

Joan: Yes.

Eric: How did you feel overall at that time, the most specific memories of how you felt? What were they?

Joan: I felt so full of hope and joy and romance. It was, I think, the last time in my life that I felt so purely optimistic about everything.

Eric: All three summers?

Joan: All three summers. Particularly the last summer when they crowned me Gypsy Princess. It was sort of like the validation of this belief that life was joyful.

63

Eric: Now in that section of your play you want to feel hope and joy and romantic idealism.

Joan: And at the same time a kind of sadness because it isn't there anymore. I want to stimulate the feelings of hope and joy and then realize that they're gone.

Eric: Okay. Now, using the Self Inventory, go back over your list of sensory stimuli—the middy uniform, the lodge at night, and so on, and what you might do is first get an overall sense of how these things make you feel. Then if they seem to be taking you in the right direction, select one of them and work sensorily on a more specific level and see if it takes you where you want to go. You may find some even more poignant elements than what's on your list, but it all starts with the Self Inventory.

Joan: Eric, what I might try is in that Swan Lake section, when I'm in the doctor's office. I might work for being in the pine woods at Four Winds, wildflowers all around, the sun and the air—I remember the air had a mixture of chill and hot. It was like wine on my skin and I could surround myself in the doctor's office with this sensory element of that past time . . .

Eric: And the fact that you are no longer in your teens and you're not in that place should stimulate the sadness you want in the scene.

Joan: Yes, I think it will.

Eric: One thing I want to add to that, caution you about. What makes it there and then specifically at that time? Was it a particular smell only indigenous to there? Was it a particular feeling related only to that place, to that time? Otherwise, it may be a conglomeration of many experiences. It has to be specified. Taking Self Inventory, dealing with sensory elements, you must specify what makes it that particular thing.

Joan: Because a conglomerate thing is general, right?

Eric: Right. What you want is the purity of a specific response.

GETTING RELATED TO PEOPLE
ON AND OFF THE STAGE

Since acting usually takes place in a situation between two or more people, a vital part of Getting Ready to Get Ready is learning how to relate to people and overcoming the obstacles that prevent you from relating freely. The exercises in this section all deal with relationship, either between two people or between an individual and a group. These exercises are neither busy work for beginning actors nor idle gymnastics to keep yourself limber between jobs. On the contrary, they apply directly to the craft of acting and are most effective when done "under fire"—that is, in actual rehearsals of plays or on a movie set.

Among professional actors there is a stigma attached to doing "exercises" on the job. So-called pros frown on bringing the classroom to the set and the serious actor has to hide behind scenery to do his preparations. This attitude is part of a tradition of slick professionalism and cool, impersonal acting. But art is totally personal and rehearsals should be designed to reveal and enhance each artist's unique contribution to the material.

You can't deny your feelings in life and then turn a switch when you get on stage and magically become a free, colorfully expressive actor. As we've said before and will say again, the approach is far more than a way for work. It is a way of life. It has to be, otherwise it won't work for you when you get on stage. If directors would lead their casts through some of these exercises, if they would dare to ruffle some of the feathers, they would get results in their final products that would far outstrip the cardboard cutouts we now see in theatre. Audiences would begin to see the difference between reality and imitation and actors would begin to demand their right to use rehearsal time creatively to encourage the infinite variety of life that comes out of BEING. Instead, what usually goes on in rehearsals are the social amenities and the niceties. All this social concern prevents people from exploring their inner lives, which is where the gold is.

THE ROUND EXERCISES

There are a number of Rounds with several different emphases, but all of the Rounds are done with the people sitting in a circle so that everyone can see everyone else. The Rounds originated in class where they've been used for eight years with impressive results, but they can also be used in a rehearsal group.

Actors in scenes often relate to each other generally, fearing really to affect each other. The Round demands a greater degree of honesty in relating; more specific exposure of what you really feel without hiding behind a character. You are only speaking for you. Over a period of time, as you practice the Rounds, you become more specific and personal and that carries into your acting. The Rounds help you eliminate the separation between you and the character.

The basic purpose of these Round Exercises is to stimulate relationship on an honest, organic, one-to-one, one-to-three, one-to-eight level. Another purpose is to get to know yourself better through the eyes of others. Also you learn to overcome your social reluctance and the fear of expressing so-called negative emotions. You allow yourself to experience conflict with other people, which is inherent in most dramatic material but which our conditioning teaches us to avoid. By taking responsibility for all that you feel, you get deeper into your inner life.

I've found that, in class, the Rounds produce love, affection and concern among the actors and I'm convinced the same thing would happen in a rehearsal group.

33. Ego Reconstruction

Sitting in a circle, observe and perceive the people around you. Whether it's your first time in the group or whether you know the people well, express to individuals your perception of them in a way that you feel would be constructive or helpful to their growth. For example: "You know, Sandra, I get the feeling that you don't really listen to what people say to you . . . Joe, in the last couple of weeks you seem so open and warm, it's a pleasure to look at you . . ." etc.

Be careful to avoid two-way conversations or it degenerates into a coffee klatch. It's easy to lose control of this exercise. Whether you agree or disagree with what's said to you, just listen.

66

Naturally, there will be a degree of subjectivity and bias in what's said. Some women are prettier than others, some actors work more than others and there's jealousy. But for the most part, people are surprisingly affirmative in this exercise. And if the actor hears the same kind of things said to him over a period of time, he begins to accept that what has been said to him is valid. If a pretty but mousey actress hears often enough that she is pretty, she may soon accept that as a reality.

The exercise is as beneficial for the person expressing the observation as it is to the one hearing it.

When we do it in class, I impose two limitations: you may not be cruel for the sake of being cruel. And you may not violate anybody's privacy without permission. The leader of the Round is responsible for enforcing these rules.

34. Reluctancy

The word is neither correct nor a typographical error. Over the years I've coined words and made up words that have a special meaning to me and my students because they communicate what I want to say better than the right word.

A Reluctancy is the expression of anything you feel uncomfortable about, anything that's difficult for you to say publicly, things you feel ashamed of, afraid of, uptight about or reluctant to express for any reason. The exercise is done in the round and for the sake of guidelines, we've used the following categories: Self, Encounter, Physical and Sexual. There are many other areas you can use. These categories should not restrict you. Any kind of reluctancy is right for the exercise.

Self Reluctancy is the expression of anything that is about *you.* "I am reluctant to open my mouth . . . I'm reluctant to say anything . . . I feel I'm going to make an ass out of myself . . . I'm ashamed to admit that I wish I weren't a mother, I wish my children were gone and I could be free . . ."

Encounter Reluctancy is anything you feel reticent about saying to another person in the room. "I'm really very attracted to you, Mary. How do you feel about me?" (Mary shouldn't answer at this point, because two-way conversations disintegrate the exercise) . . ."Karl, you hurt my feelings when you walked in the room tonight and passed right by me without saying anything . . . Pete, I'm sick of your whining. If you really want what you say you want, get up off your ass and go get it . . . "

Physical Reluctancy is the exposure of anything about your body that concerns you or anything you are physically reluctant to do. For instance, you might feel proud of your physique but reluctant to get up and take off your shirt and flex your muscles. In this exercise you would encourage yourself to do it. Or you might feel that you're overweight and have a fat belly that you're ashamed of and so you'd get up and expose it and talk about how it affects you. Or you might want to touch someone, but feel afraid of their response. In this exercise you would carry out that action. (The only limitation here is against violating another person's rights. You're not allowed to assault someone sexually or hurt anyone.)

Sexual Reluctancy is anything sexual you feel reluctant to express. For example, in one class a student said he was very uptight about the size of his penis. He said it's about five and a half inches and he wished it were bigger . . . Rosemary admitted she fakes orgasms . . . Others have expressed fear of first sexual encounters, anxiety about being able to get or maintain an erection.

Reluctancy is a training exercise. It should not be used in a casual rehearsal group. The exercise can be dangerous unless it is led by a skillful and responsible leader in a group where the people meet regularly. When it works well, it is exciting, sometimes explosive, often funny and always freeing. If you do this exercise over a period of time, it progressively opens more doors of expression. The inhibitions you started with disappear and this freedom carries directly into your acting. The more you expose youself in Reluctancy and in your life, the more areas are open to you on the stage and the more personal is your expression in a piece of material. Reluctancy teaches you that you need not fear the skeletons in your closet. Everybody has them and it's okay. Many actors are free in some areas, but totally closed in others. Reluctancy is designed to open all your doors. It encourages you to relate to other people very personally from the center of your own being, and your relationships on stage are honest and real. The fear that what you feel and express on stage will be taken personally, and yourself held responsible for it, stops most actors. They hide behind the lines and the character and if it gets hot, they cop out by saying, "That isn't me. That's the character." There is only *you.* There is no character. The character is you.

35. How I See Myself

This exercise is also done in the round, but it is done individually. The person doing the exercise is either called on by the leader, or volunteers to do it. You need not get up and stand in the center, because the exercise is "spot"-producing enough as it is. In anywhere from two minutes to ten, talk about how you see yourself and think of yourself. *Not* the way you think other people perceive you, but the way *you* feel you are. The trap to avoid in the exercise is the second-guessing of what other people might think of you. Stay true to your *self* image.

For instance, "I see myself as being very intelligent. When people meet me for the first time, I can see immediately that they know I'm intelligent. I'm articulate. I think a lot, I think an awful lot. I feel I'm pretty attractive. I've got a groovy body, I've got a good personality and when I get excited, I feel I'm a very exciting person. I feel I'm sexually attractive and women relate to me very well and I'm talented, far more talented than I've ever to this point been able to release. I like people. I like to relate to people. I'm good at that. I feel I'm moody sometimes. I get depressed and very low, and when I'm like that I often alienate people . . . . "

Try to cover all facets of yourself. When you're finished, ask for feedback from the group. Say to them, "Is the way I see myself consistent or inconsistent with the way you see me?" The feedback can come from as many as seven or eight people, depending on time. In my two-day marathons, I allow all those who want to give feedback to give it, no matter how long it takes.

In giving feedback, a person might say, "Yeah, I think you're intelligent and I think you think a lot, but I don't think you're *expressive* of what you think . . . I would like to hear more of what you think. You think too much.

Someone else might say, "I agree that you're sexually attractive, but you withhold it. To me you come across cold."

Sometimes a person's self image is delusional, totally based on fantasy. Feedback from the group makes him aware of the gap between his self image and the reality.

Everyone doing the Self Image will receive enough responses to make a valid cross-reference of what is true. The exercise is invaluable for dealing with the inconsistencies between what you think

"Two-People Relationship" exercise.

you are and what you actually are. You might be everything you think you are, but very little of it is being expressed. You may feel that your relationships to people on and off the stage are very full and free, but in fact you may learn in the exercise that this isn't true. The feedback will direct you specifically to areas that you need work in.

36. Feedback

Although Feedback is used in Self Image, this exercise is separate from it. Again it's done in the round and also on an individual basis, but this time it's strictly voluntary. If you want Feedback, you ask for it. There are two ways you can do it. The first way is based on George Bach's mind-reading exercise and goes something like this: "Joe, I think you think I'm abstract and complicated and don't understand what I'm talking about and I become mystical and abstract to hide the truth, which is that I really don't know what I'm talking about. Is that what you think?"

Then Joe answers you, and he might say, "I never thought any of that. I don't know where you got that." Or he might say, "Yeah, I think you are very complicated and I think you do make things more difficult to understand than they have to be, but it *isn't* because I think you don't know what you're talking about."

Now the second kind is when you ask a person for Feedback in a specific area. "Joan, what do you think of me as a teacher? Do you think I'm patient and understanding with people?" And Joan might say, "Yes, I think you're very patient." Or she might say, "No, I think you could be more patient with some people."

You might ask, "Sue, what do you think of me as an actor?" And Sue might answer, "What do you mean what do I think of you as an actor? Do you mean do I think you're talented, or do I think you're a particular kind of actor, or do you need work in certain areas?" The person being asked for Feedback can demand more specificity. Then you might ask Sue, "Okay, what do you think of my work recently. Do you think I've grown as an actor?" Now that's specific. And Sue could answer, "The last two scenes I've seen you do—I've seen a great deal of growth. You're simpler. You're more related to the other actor. You're much less tense."

When you volunteer for this exercise, you can use either or both of these approaches. Feedback is designed to help you understand yourself better, to know if what you're perceiving is true, and also

—vitally important—the exercise encourages you to reach out to people and ask for response to you.

This kind of Round is suitable for a rehearsal group, because it can flush out those negative mind-readings that occur in rehearsals and impede the creative work. For example, the actor who thinks the director hates him, or the director who thinks the actors are laughing at him behind his back. An aspect that makes it good for a rehearsal group is that it's self-regulatory. You don't have to ask for Feedback if you don't want it.

TWO-PEOPLE RELATIONSHIP EXERCISE

These exercises can be used in a variety of situations—classroom, rehearsal group, private rehearsal between you and another actor, on a motion picture set—anywhere. They are all designed to get you related to another person, to get you *involved, related and responsive to another person.* Besides this central purpose, these exercises have additional benefits:

- To help your concentration.

- To alleviate your tension.

- To stimulate your vulnerability.

- To pique your curiosity.

- To elevate your ability to perceive and observe.

- To increase your courage by asking for what you want.

- To overcome physical inhibitions to touching another person.

- To sensitize you to the other person and what's going on with him.

- To train you to look *into* another person rather than *at* him.

37. Hold Hands and Look at Each Other

Best results when done for a long period of time, at least fifteen minutes. Two people sit and hold each other's hands comfortably and look into each other's eyes. Allow and encourage everything that happens to happen. At first, you might be embarrassed and want to look away. You might want to talk, which isn't allowed. As you continue the exercise, many feelings are expressed between you. At the end of the time, a relationship has begun which can go in any direction.

38. Two People Touch

Can be done with your eyes open or closed. No talking. Simply relate to each other by touching and feeling. You will become emotionally related as well as physically.

39. Relate As If for the First Time

A good exercise when two actors have known each other a long time and have begun taking things for granted. Approach the exercise by first looking at your partner as if you've never seen him or her before. Actually search for things which you have honestly never noticed before. Use all of your senses together in the same way, discovering things you've never been aware of. Talking is allowed if you feel like it. Really listen for sounds and intonations that are new to you. This emphasis will stimulate a kind of first-time relationship and will freshen your rehearsal with many new facets of behavior and responses. Instead of taking each other for granted, you will become unpredictable to each other and eventually to an audience.

40. Ask for What You Want

A two-people exercise which can also be done in a group. As it says in the title, that's what you do. You ask the other person for what you want from him or her. The success of the exercise depends on how courageous you are in really exposing your needs. The trap here is to make small talk—"What did you do today? . . . I want to know what you did before you came here. . ." Instead of *really* asking for what you want. "Do you like me? . . . How do you feel about me? . . . I wish we could be closer than we are . . . I want you to be more sensitive to my feelings."

The other person can reply if he wishes, or choose not to. Each person does it until he's finished asking for everything he wants. Then the other person does it.

41. Double Exposure

This is an exercise designed to get two people related personally, as all the exercises in this part of the chapter are meant to do. Double Exposure helps you relate to the other person *personally.* That word can't be stressed too much. *Personally.* It is done either standing or sitting. Look at each other and progressively expose more personal things about yourself to the other actor. The actors take turns speaking and listening. It should not be a dialogue. Two-way conversation is discouraged, although you can ask each other for clarification if you don't understand something. Start simply and become more personal with each exposure. Don't violate your privacy or anybody else's. There is a definite line between what is personal and what is private. Don't expose anything that can hurt you or anyone else such as names, dates, places and facts that can be incriminating in any way. The line between what is private and what is personal varies among individuals, but if your line of what is private includes *everything,* then you're not being *personal!*

42. Telepathy

Not an ESP exercise. It's called Telepathy because it demands that two people communicate without words, pantomime or charade-type gestures. It encourages them to reach deeply into each other to try to find out what's going on. What is the other person trying to communicate? You may never find out what he's telling you, but the *reaching* is what's important in Telepathy.

Sit or stand close enough to each other to make physical contact. Start with your eyes closed. Have an intent and try to communicate it to the other person through your body and, at the same time, try to receive his message. Holding hands, you can express a lot to each other just by the energies flowing through, but it's important that you express yourself through all parts of your body. After a while, open your eyes and continue giving and receiving impulses without words or illustrative gestures. You may use non-verbal sounds.

You'll find you'll be much more involved with the other actor than before and less dependent on words to express that involvement. Your relationship will occur on subtler levels of behavior and have more dimension than if you had started with words. Telepathy is a good exercise to start a rehearsal. The next logical step would be to begin working with the choices you're using in the scene.

43. Observe, Wonder and Perceive II

This is the two-people version. The exercise has already been described in the section on Awareness, but here it's used to stimulate relationship and not only to get you related to the other actor, but to get you involved with each other and ready to work. You can do it in any physical position as long as you can look at each other. Observe, perceive and wonder about the other actor. That means anything that you see, hear, feel, taste or smell. You will observe things that are obviously there—"I observe that you're sitting down and putting your hands in your lap." You'll perceive behind what is obviously there—a fleeting look in the eye, a subtle gesture which might be protective or defensive and you might deduce, "I perceive from your behavior that you're getting ready to do this exercise and you're a little uncomfortable." Then you encourage the things that you truly wonder about—"I wonder if you're uncomfortable because of the exercise or because of me." Mostly you'll wonder about things that you perceive sensorily. You might feel the texture of the person's cashmere jacket and wonder if he's wealthy. You might pick up a scent of cologne mixed with perspiration and wonder if she put the cologne on without taking a bath, or if she's just very nervous at the moment.

Allow your observations, perceptions and wonderments to be kicked off by all your five senses and to go where they will:

"I wonder why he's so stiff. He really looks uptight. He wears an awful lot of jewelry. I wonder why. I hear an accent. I wonder where he's from. He's kind of social and phony, all that politeness. I wonder what he's really thinking and feeling. He doesn't show anything. What would he do if I told him I think he's a phony? I just saw something—he lost his cool for a minute. I saw fear in his face. It even affected his voice, there's a faint tremor there . . . " etc., etc.

You can do the exercise silently or semi-audibly or out loud. The reason for doing it semi-audibly is to take you out of your head by verbalizing your responses so that you can hear them, although

Two-people Being is a four-part exercise: 1) Deal with the Demons. 2) Observe — Wonder — Perceive your partner. 3) Work for a simple sensory choice. 4) Obligate yourself to a specific feeling.

your partner can't. The advantage of doing it out loud is that it stimulates a verbal relationship, an involvement that gets you out of yourself, off the spot and into each other. The only caution is to avoid a gab session which would distract you from rehearsing. Stay with your observations, perceptions and wonderments.

44. Two-People *BEING*

This is a four-part exercise. I started using it in class regularly to promote the state of BEING. The exercise is preparation—getting ready to work with another person, getting ready to do a rehearsal, getting ready to do a scene. Two people stand in front of a group, either a rehearsal group or a class or in an audition. It's important that the two people doing the exercise remain standing throughout, because it intensifies the feeling of being on the spot.

In the first part, both actors express semi-audibly in stream-of-consciousness style all their anxieties and tensions about being in front of the group, all their awareness of what's going on. No one hears the actor, but the actor hears himself. He must actually say what he's thinking to avoid an inner head game. "I'm standing here and I see the people looking at me. They're all looking at me as if they expect something and that intimidates me. Joanne is staring at me and I feel she's hostile and it makes me uptight. Joe just walked out. Maybe I'm boring to him. I'm afraid of being dull. Gee, I have a lot of tension in the back of my neck . . . I feel better now. I still have some tension, but it's okay. I feel I could get involved with my partner."

Once you have acknowledged and "dealt with the demons," expurgated some of your tension and become more comfortable in relation to the audience, you go to the second part of the exercise, which is to Observe-Wonder-Perceive your partner. Do this in the same way as described in the exercise above.

When you feel sufficiently involved with your partner, go to the third part. (Throughout the entire exercise you continue to acknowledge and express anything that intrudes upon your awareness, such as a creeping tension or people moving in the audience and your concern about that.) In the third part, work for a simple sensory choice in relation to your partner without obligating yourself to any result. We'll explain in detail later how to work for a sensory choice. You might try to create eyeglasses on your partner or a mustache or different color hair or bad breath or a certain look in his eyes that doesn't now exist. The purpose here is to get you started on the sensory process and to prime you to take on an emotional obligation, as in a scene.

If you are doing this exercise as preparation for doing a scene, now is the time you start working for your first choice in that scene. And that's the fourth part. If you're using it just as a BEING exercise, then in this fourth part you obligate yourself to something you want to feel in relation to your partner, such as jealousy, desire, compassion, fear, etc. Make the obligation very clear to yourself. It's not just general jealousy or general fear. Make clear to yourself what you're jealous about. Then make a sensory choice that you think might stimulate that particular kind of jealousy and work for it, going *wherever* the choice takes you.

The BEING exercise is designed to get you in touch with who you are, what you feel, how you're functioning in terms of here and now. That reality is the only place you can act from. There isn't any other place you can act from organically.

45. Rock and Stroke

Two people sit on the floor. One person cradles the other in his lap, as you might do with a small child, and rocks him gently, petting and stroking and possibly humming a lullaby. Both people should totally give themselves to this exercise, which is non-verbal. After five or ten minutes, the rocker becomes the rockee and vice versa. It is not a sexual exercise. Men can do it with men and women with women.

The visible results of this exercise are startling. People really change during that time. They become mellow, soft, open, warm and loving. The exercise pushes some kind of primal button, the basic need to be held and stroked. It's a marvelous exercise for starting a rehearsal or ending a rehearsal, for starting or ending a class.

Getting Ready to Get Ready is a preparation to prepare. Far too many actors think of preparation as getting ready to do the scene or a specific piece of material, and that is where they start. There is a mandatory step before this one, however, and that deals with making your instrument ready to receive input. This pre-preparation is related to reaching an authentic BEING state; eliminating the tension, sensitizing, getting in touch with everything you feel and opening the doors to expression. The exercises in this chapter will help you only if they are learned, practiced and applied on a daily, living basis. You can't read a book and learn how to act, but once you start applying these exercises you will experience their accumulative results. Each time you repeat an exercise, using it in all phases of your life and your work, you will become progressively more skilled at recognizing and alleviating your tension, increasing your awareness and bringing it to the stage. Knowing the component parts of who you are and using yourself on and off the stage, and finally, getting related to other people is what life and theatre are all about.

Sense memory takes place in the senses, not in the head.

Chapter

3

COMMON SENSORY ACTING

SENSE MEMORY

Throughout my years of teaching, actors have come to me from all kinds of training; actors who have been Method-trained, actors who have not been Method-trained, actors who have brushed with the concept of sense memory and actors who believed they knew sense memory well. Some have even been pompously defensive of their knowledge and usage of it. My experience has been that most actors do not understand the concept of sense memory and do not know how to use it. They confuse sensory work with pantomime and intellectual gymnastics, neither of which works in creating realities on stage. These actors have come from all the well-established Method teachers in the country, so obviously sense memory is either not being communicated clearly, or it isn't being understood. Because it is misunderstood and misused, it is maligned in the business as "Method masturbation."

There are two areas of confusion and misunderstanding. First, most people think that sense memory is an intellectual process and it is not. It does not take place in the head. It takes place in the senses. And second, it's not something you can do once and expect it to work. Once you truly understand the *how* of sense memory, you must practice it daily to make it your own, to make it work for you. You do it for yourself. It's your way of creating realities which you personally respond to and which change your life to match the character's life on the stage.

Linda Crystal in a class.

As a teacher I've found that it's essential to be repetitiously specific about how to do the sense memory exercise. And it's equally essential that the actor then take on the responsibility of practicing it daily, weekly, monthly, yearly. Sense memory is one tool in a large tool box. It's not your only tool, but it's an important one. An actor's job is to bring to the stage a human being with a full set of emotions and behavior patterns, a living person who is as unpredictable to see himself as he is to the audience that has paid to see him. The circumstances of any drama require the actor to respond to realities which are not real at all. The actress playing his sister is not really his sister. The palace walls are made out of unbleached muslin. He must train his instrument to respond to these imaginary objects as if they really existed by making them real to himself.

We are all a composite of everything that has come in through one or more of our five sensory doors—seeing, hearing, feeling, tasting, smelling. Everything we've ever experienced has found its path into our consciousness through our senses and has stimulated some kind of behavior. So it's only common sense to return to your senses to stimulate your behavior on stage. We feel something about everything and everything stimulates some kind of behavior in us. Sense memory is the ability to re-create, through your senses, the object that affected you and impelled you to behave in a certain way.

Before we go into the process of learning to sense memorize an object, we'll give you at this point a couple of preparatory exercises for discovering your senses. It's very important for you to find out how your senses work, and to be on intimate terms with your personal instrument, because later, when you start on sense memory, you'll know what kinds of questions appeal to your senses. You'll be able to frame the questions that specifically awaken your senses and avoid a lot of academic questions that don't really apply to your apparatus.

1. Sensory Inventory

Read again the description of this exercise on Page 55 in Chapter II, and explore it daily, adding your own discoveries to it as you go along. Approach it as if it were an adventure.

80

2. The Sensory Game

Allot certain times in the day to play this game and have fun with it. Use all of your senses and encourage them to relate to all of the real objects around you, asking yourself all kinds of questions. While you're eating, for instance, ask yourself how many different tastes you're aware of and how many sounds you hear around you. Look at the room you're in. How many things do you see? How many different colors can you find? Notice all of the objects that have been there a long time which you haven't paid any attention to. At the same time, take an emotional inventory and ask yourself how you feel about each object. You probably won't have a large emotional response to most objects, but you'll find that you feel *something* about everything. Look around any room for two minutes and then close your eyes and try to reconstruct the room. Then open your eyes and see what you missed. Run your hand over every object in a room and ask questions about the different textures. How is wood different from cloth? What's the difference between the rug and the drapes? And how do I feel about those drapes? Pick up objects which you wouldn't ordinarily taste and then taste them—a lampshade, a cigarette box, a flower. The idea is to have fun and make it exciting.

That picture of your girlfriend or boyfriend—when was it taken? Do you recall the clothes you wore that day? Who else was there? Was it a hot day or rainy and cold? You'll never run out of questions to ask yourself. You might suddenly be taken back to another time and place and re-experience the same kinds of feelings you had then. You might find a little reminiscent smile on your lips . . . Well, that's living. That's an emotional experience which started by looking at a picture and asking yourself a few questions.

As you practice the Sensory Game, you'll become much more observant in your daily life and sensorily alive, as well as increasingly aware of your personal point of view. At first, when you do this exercise, your questions will be general, but after a while, they'll become more complex and you'll be involved in sensory subtleties. Your questions about how you feel toward these objects will grow more complex as well. Encourage yourself to express those feelings. Be quite deliberate about it. If it's a piece of music that makes you feel like dancing, then dance! If it's an odor that offends you, voice your displeasure. The Game deals only with real objects, but be assured that after you play it awhile, your senses will become just as willing to respond to imaginary objects.

There are no rules except to use all your senses. Make it your own private game and you will find yourself playing it more and more often. Remember the most creative actors are the actors who have the most fun in their work.

JELLYBEAN:

Nothing Is Something

APPLICATION OF SENSE MEMORY

The application of sense memory to acting lies in the fact that it trains you to create realities that really don't exist. In a play or a scene, those realities are the place, the character, your relationship to the other person and the emotional life you must feel according to the circumstances of the material. If you can create a cup of coffee successfully in your hand when it does not exist, create it so that you can taste, smell, feel, see and hear it, then you can create the stimuli that will make you feel those things which the play demands of the character. For example, if your obligation is to be lonely, you can create a place that you have really been lonely in, surrounding yourself with objects that stimulate the feelings of loneliness in you. You can do that here and now, on the stage, so that *you* are really as lonely as the character in the play. The only difference between the character and the actor is the objects that stimulate the loneliness. You and the character become one. But it all starts with the cup of coffee. If you can't create the coffee, you can't create the place or the loneliness.

3.   The Sense Memory Exercise

The importance of the Sense Memory Exercise cannot be overstated. It is the cornerstone of the craftual foundation. It's a wise decision to choose to work with something to eat or to drink, because this type of object involves all five of your senses. For practice purposes, always use an object that makes demands on all the senses, because then you are constantly exercising your total instrument. Later, when you're using sense memory in your choice work, you can isolate one sense for a specific reason. You might want to create a piece of music, using the auditory sense, or work for an odor, which is olfactory. But for now, while you're practicing, it's like practicing scales on the piano and you should practice by exercising all five senses.

After you've selected your object—a glass of milk, a cup of coffee, a piece of candy or fruit—find yourself a place to go to do your work. It should be a comfortable place with a minimum of distractions. It's a good habit to establish a place of work.

Start with any of your five senses. Very soon you'll know which of your five senses is the strongest. Use it to encourage the others to respond. Suppose your object is a cup of coffee. From this point forward, get in the habit of referring to *any* object you work with as "the object" and not by its name. Names and descriptive labels tend to *suggest* a sensory response rather than evoking it purely in the sense itself. Descriptive words supply your senses with the answer instead of piquing them to respond by themselves. The kinds of answers you want are non-verbal and lie in your fingers, your ears, your tongue, your eyes—not in language. There is no language in sense memory. Our senses are conditioned to be lazy through non-use and they will go to sleep on you unless you appeal to them specifically through no-name words. *Temperature,* not hot or cold. *Object,* not cup or orange. *Size,* not inches or feet. *Texture,* not rough or smooth. *Color,* not red or blue.

Having selected your object, a cup of coffee with cream and sugar, because cream and sugar add visual and taste elements (but if you must have it black, okay), you're ready to begin the exercise. The order of your physical action will be to place the cup of coffee on the table, lift the cup to your mouth, take a swallow and put it back on the table. Simple as that sounds, it may take you hundreds of questions and two weeks of daily practice before you even get the cup to your mouth. You're about to embark on an amazing adventure.

Start with the visual sense. The cup is on the table. Begin by locating it in space with a *spatial* question:

- Where is the object on the table?

Respond to that question with your eyes. It is where you see it is. Then support that first spatial question with other questions in the same category:

● How far from the right edge of the table does the object sit? Look and see.

● How far is it from the left edge of the table?

Again, respond visually. It is as far from the left edge of the table as your eyes *see* it is. Avoid all language-type answers, such as inches or feet. It is only as far from the left edge of the table as your eyes tell you it is.

● What's the distance between the object and me?

Let your eyes respond.

● How much of the table area does the object cover?

● How wide is the object?

● How high does it stand off the table?

Remember, the only answers are your visual responses, what your eyes see and tell you. No words. When asking how high it stands off the table, you might compare it to another object on the table. For instance, there might be a lamp on your table. You could ask:

● How high off the table is the object compared to the lamp? (It's all right to give label names to other objects that you're not working on.)

This kind of comparative question further supports the spatial relationship of your object, because when you begin to work *without* the object, these points of comparison help you to locate it in space.

It's important to note that when you ask a categorical question (space is a category), you must support that question with others in the same category rather than skip to another category altogether. For instance, if you ask, "Where is the object?" And then you ask, "What is the color?"—those are two questions from different categories and you've not encouraged your senses to respond to the first question by specifying other questions in that same area of exploration.

There are many other questions you can ask in the spatial category. For example, you might now involve another sense, the tactile, by asking:

- In reaching my hand and arm toward the object, what is the distance that my arm has to travel to make contact with the object?

The purpose of all these questions is to put the object some place in space so that, when you're working without it, you have a definite, specific relationship to where the object was and can re-create it when you're working for the imaginary object.

In any category you can ask twenty, thirty, forty, two thousand questions, depending on your imagination and depending on what the object itself suggests to you, because different objects suggest different questions. It's important for you to realize that the questions are endless. We're giving you seven or eight and you can take it from there. For instance, another spatial question might be:

- If I were to lean back at eye level with the object, how much of the wall behind it does the object obscure?

You can stand up and look down on the object and, in looking down at it, ask:

- From this position, where exactly in relation to the *center* of the table does the object sit?

Invent your own questions. After you've asked six to ten questions working with the object, put the object aside. Be sure it's entirely out of your view. In trying to re-create the imaginary object, you don't want the real object even in your peripheral view because it will confuse your senses.

Then ask the same group of questions over again and try to respond sensorily to the imaginary object, encouraging yourself to get a sense of its really being there. If other spatial questions that you haven't asked before occur to you now, ask them. Feel free to ask questions that you haven't asked before, if they come to mind, and try to respond visually to those questions. When you've done this, put the real object back in the exact position it was in. Take a quick inventory of where you succeeded in getting responses, where you didn't, and what you may have forgotten.

Now, with the real object in front of you again, ask another group of questions. At this point you may want to involve the tactile sense, since you've already asked a visual-tactile question about reaching for the object. Your question might be:

- As I get close to the object with four fingers and thumb, do I begin to anticipate contact anywhere in my hand?

- Do I have any feeling in my fingertips about the anticipated contact?

Answer the questions in those parts of your fingertips where you get even a tingle of response.

- How close does my hand come to the object before I feel any temperature?

You might feel the heat of your own body bounce off the object and this is a meaningful response.

- As I come closer and closer to the object with all my fingers, at what point on the object and at what point on the finger do I first make contact?

This is a triple question, a three-in-one, involving both visual and tactile. Give yourself enough time in each sense to respond. Let yourself *see* the point of contact on the object. Let yourself *see* the point of contact on your finger. And *feel* the point of contact on the finger.

- What do I feel in that finger?

The answer to a question about feeling is the sensation in that part of each finger and thumb which has made contact with the object.

- What do I feel as I make contact with the other fingers of that hand?

- At how many points on my fingers have I made contact?

- Still touching the object lightly, what does it feel like?

"Like" means, "What do my fingers interpret as they feel it?" Don't answer in simile. Answer with the tactile sense. It feels like what it feels like. After any group of questions you may stop and work without the object, taking inventory of what you missed or forgot, then continue working with the real object. Also, if you want, you may ask the same question over and over again, working with and without the object, in order to develop specificity in that one part of a particular sense.

- What is the texture of the object?

Texture is a supportive question in the category of what it feels like. Texture can also be its own category.

- What is the difference between what I feel texturally in each finger?

Give each finger time to respond individually, because each finger may, in fact, respond to that texture differently. There's the possibility that the temperature affects the texture at different points on the object. Your little finger might be lower down on the object than your middle finger or your index finger and because the liquid might be at a different temperature at the lower portion of the object, your little finger might experience moisture, which would affect the texture.

- Keeping my fingers in one place, do I feel a textural difference in any one of them?

- Is there moisture?

- If so, where?

- How does the sensation of moisture differ from the areas of no moisture?

Let your fingers find out all the answers. Don't say to yourself, "It's dry there, it's hot there, it's cold there, it's wet there."

- Without moving my fingers, do I feel any irregularities?

- If so, how do my fingers know this?

- Can I feel the shape of the object?

Now at this point you might include two or three visual questions:

- What is the overall shape of the object?

- What is the difference between the shape at the top and at the bottom?

- How much wider does it look at the top than at the bottom?

- Where the sides taper, how steep is the angle?

Then piggyback your visual questions with some tactile ones:

- How does the visual shape differ from what I feel?

- Can I feel the shape?

- Do my fingers feel that taper?

- What is the temperature?

Answer with one finger at a time. Encourage each finger to respond individually. Your questions can weave back and forth between visual and tactile. Suppose there's steam rising from the coffee. You've just experienced the temperature in your fingertips. You might support that with visual clues to the object's temperature:

- Is there steam rising?

- If so, what shape does it take?

- Can I see any designs in the shapes?

Then return to the tactile exploration:

In every Sense Memory Exercise you'll make many discoveries. This is how you'll grow as a craftsman. You'll find out what kinds of questions appeal to your senses and to your emotions. This discovery you made about the temperature is important and valuable. You learned that your body adjusts to temperature very quickly and your first response to temperature is your best. Similarly, in the olfactory area, your nose will overload quickly, numbing itself to all smells, and you'll have to walk away from the object repeatedly and return to it fresh. So now, pour yourself a fresh cup of coffee and go on.

- What is the temperature?

- In which finger do I feel it most pronounced?

- Is it different—NOT hotter, warmer, cooler—is it DIFFERENT from my own body temperature?

- What tells me?

- Is the difference uniform or is there a difference in each finger?

- With my hand in this position, touching the object, has the temperature changed?

- Has my body acclimated to it?

- If so, what does that feel like progressively?

Your hand may have to repeat the action of contact and with-drawal several times to get the answer, because once your fingers and the object have reached the same temperature, you no longer feel the difference. The time it takes for your body to acclimate itself to the object happens rather quickly and in order to sense memorize that response you may have to do it as many as a dozen times before you're able to re-create that interval.

- Are my fingers sweaty?

- Do I feel more moisture between me and the object than when I started?

- How does the light affect the object? What are the contrasts and highlights?

You're back to the visual sense now.

- Is there a reflection of the light in the liquid? Where?

- How deep does the light affect the texture of the receptacle (cup) and the liquid (coffee)?

You may take a sensory trip on this one question of how the light affects the liquid. Out of this one question may come twenty or thirty more about the designs and shapes and hues in the mixture of cream and coffee as the light affects it. It's fine to take these trips, because they were sparked by the object and piqued your interest. But after a while it's important to return to the chronology of the exercise.

- How does the light affect the shape of the object?

- Are there any distortions? What kind? Where?

- Does the light have an effect on the overall color of the object? Is the color different in the darker portions than it is in the lighter parts?

- In looking at the object can I tell where the source of light is, where it's coming from?

- Is the object casting a shadow?

- What is the length of the shadow?

- Shape of the shadow? Is there more than one shape?

- What pictures do I see in that one shape?

- Does it remind me of anything? Does it suggest anything?

Encourage these kinds of imaginative and inventive questions. The more imaginative and inventive you are, the more fun sense memory becomes. And if it's fun, you'll practice more often.

There is no specific number of questions you should ask before you work without the object. Ask as many questions at one time as you can comfortably repeat when working without the object. However, you might want to ask only one question, going back and forth between real and imaginary until you have satisfied the sensory response. After you have been doing sense memory for a time you will develop your own patterns of exploration. Remember after you've worked with the object, then you work without the object, asking yourself the same sensory questions. Again you go back to the real object to cross-check and see what you missed. The entire process is designed so you can ultimately create that cup of coffee, in total, when it is not really there.

Also, while you're practicing your Sense Memory Exercises, it's very important to BE. As you know by now, that means you include everything in your work, all your thoughts and impulses and allow yourself to express them freely. If it's tedium you're experiencing, put that feeling into the questions you ask. Life goes on no matter what you're doing—a scene, a film or a clinical scale-playing exercise.

As you do sense memory work, skip around, intermingling your various senses. You could ask three or four visual questions, two or three tactile questions, maybe go back to the visual and pick up where you left off, then ask a couple of olfactory questions, a couple of auditory ones. The sum total might come to twelve or thirteen altogether before you remove the object and work without it. It is encouraged that you intermingle your senses, use them all, but this will always depend on how advanced you are in your sense memory work, how long you've been working with this particular object and whether or not you're purposely isolating a sense and concentrating on it because it's weak and needs extra work.

On the other hand, for various reasons you may work best if you ask ten or twelve visual questions, then ten or twelve tactile questions, because perhaps it takes that many questions to get your senses to start responding. That may be the way you choose to approach the exercise and that's all right. But ultimately what you want to do is to use your senses interrelatedly so that one sense picks up its cue from another. When perceiving an object sensorily, we often get three responses at the same time—we see it, hear it and smell it simultaneously. So this is what you want to have happen with imaginary objects. Get into the habit of using the totality of your sensory apparatus. You can easily create sensory dependencies by leaning too heavily on one sense and neglecting the others.

Now suppose you're ready to pick up the cup, to lift it to your mouth and taste the coffee. You've already investigated it tactually and your hand is still on the cup. You want to grasp it so that you can lift it. You might start with questions like:

- As I apply pressure from my fingers to the object, what muscles do I feel tensing?

- What muscles in each finger?

- In my hand?

- In my wrist?

- In my arm?

- Where in my arm?

- How far up my arm do I feel the tension and pressure?

Give yourself time to identify the actual sensations in each part of your hand and arm, because when you're working without the object, the success of re-creating it depends on all those sensations.

- As I squeeze my fingers together, how much resistance does the object offer?

- How hard must I squeeze in order to grasp the object so that it won't slip through my fingers?

- How does the resistance of the object affect the tension in my fingers?

- As I press into the object, how does the object penetrate into my fingerpads? Visual and tactile—I see it and I feel it.

- How much of each finger is obscured by the object in relation to the angle I'm sitting in?

As you were working for the pressure of the object in your fingers, it became obvious to you that there were fingers you couldn't see. So this last question presented itself and you dealt with it. Always respect the chronology of sensory elements that occur while you're working and answer them. To ignore these questions when they come up would vilate the natural reality.

- Into which finger do I feel the most penetration? What does that feel like?

- Can I feel bone contact? What does that feel like?

Any of these questions may demand twenty other questions to capture all the subtleties of that one question. You'll find this out when you're working without the object. You'll find out how much more specific and how many questions you need in that particular area to get a sense of the object.

- Now I feel ready to lift the object. What must I do to lift the object? What is my first movement? Where does it start?

- Does it start in the arm or in the hand?

- Where in the arm do I begin to lift upward? What does that feel like?

- As I do that, what is the first movement I see taking place in the object?

- What sounds do I hear related to the object?

- Can I hear the liquid sloshing?

- What are the component parts of that subtle sound?

- With which ear do I perceive that?

- What other sounds do I hear in the room?

- What is the predominant sound? Where is it coming from?

- As I slowly move my arm upward, how does it affect the liquid?

- As I move my hand slowly upward to lift the object, how does it tilt?

- What part of the object leaves the table first?

- Can I hear that?

- What muscles am I now using that I wasn't using before? Where do I feel them? What does it feel like?

- When do I begin to feel the increased weight now that the object is off the table?

- What is weight? What do I mean by weight in terms of what I'm feeling?

- How do I feel weight? Where in my fingers, hand, wrist and arm do I feel that thing I call weight?

- What is the downward pressure that the object exerts on my fingers, my hand, my wrist?

- How far up the arm do I feel that pull?

- As I move the object toward my face, how does the weight change?

- What other muscles come into play?

- What other pressures do I feel?

- What about the fatigue factor? I've been holding it here a long time. Where are my muscles beginning to get tired and how does that feel? What are the sensations of fatigue?

- As I move it close to my face, how much more of the liquid can I see?

- And in this new position how far down into the object can I see?

- Is the liquid moving as a result of the movement of my hand?

- Where in my hand do I feel the movement of that liquid?

- As I move the cup around in small circles, where in my hand do I feel the sloshing of the liquid?

- Can I hear that?

- What other weight changes take place as I move closer to my face?

- As I get closer, at what point do I begin to feel the temperature? Where on my face do I feel that temperature?

- Is there steam? Where do I feel it? Where does it emanate? What does it look like?

- What is the difference between the temperature of the liquid as I get it close to my face and the temperature of my face around the area that's not being affected? Can I distinguish a difference?

- At what point do I begin to smell the object?

- What is smell? Where do I smell? Where in my nose, in my nostrils, do I smell? What do I mean by smell?

- How many different odors do I detect?

- What are those differences?

- Can I smell the cream? The sugar? The coffee? The object itself?

- As I bring it closer, do I smell more?

- How many other odors am I aware of around me?

- With which nostril do I smell the most? I might have to block each nostril with my other hand to answer that question.

At any point you may want to stop and work with and without the object in small areas. For instance, when the object is closest to your face, you're seeing, smelling, feeling, hearing all at once. Your senses are being flooded with stimulation. So you might have to break it down and take it in small hunks, working separately with each sense and then putting it together.

- In lifting the object to my mouth to taste it, what is the angle of my hand? The angle of my arm? Where is my arm in relation to my shoulder? In relation to my head? Where? How high? What do I see?

- How high is my hand in relation to the height of the table?

- As I approach my mouth and begin tilting my head to receive the liquid, how far back do I tilt my head?

- What angle is my head in relation to the table?

- What do I see as my head goes back?

- As my head goes back, at what point on the ceiling do my eyes stop? What is that visual point?

- As I bring the object up to my lips, how intense does the temperature get on my lips? Where do I feel that?

- What do I see at this point, with the object so close? Is it blurred?

- What part of the cup touches my lip first?

- Which lip first? Bottom or top?

- As it touches my lip, how does it feel specifically at the contact point? How does it feel radiating outward from that point?

- Temperature? Texture? What part of the lip feels the most?

- How long does it take for the lip to get accustomed to the temperature of the object?

- As my top lip touches the object, how much difference between the top lip and the bottom? What do I feel with the top lip?

- As the liquid goes into my mouth, what part of my mouth does it hit first?

- Exactly at that moment of contact of the liquid in my mouth, what do I feel?

- What is the temperature? What is the sensation of temperature?

- What is the difference in temperature between the inside of my mouth and the liquid? What in my mouth tells me that?

- What is temperature, what is heat in terms of the feeling I'm getting in my mouth?

- What is the path of the liquid as it runs into my mouth? What parts of my mouth does it run into?

- What are the many different sensations I'm experiencing in my mouth?

- Can I smell it internally?

- As the liquid runs back into my mouth, are there any sensitive teeth? Do I feel any pain in any parts of the gums and inner cheek?

- How long does it take for the liquid to equalize to my mouth's temperature?

- What is the consistency of the liquid? What does it feel like on my tongue– what parts of my tongue?

- What are the taste sensations? Where do I begin to taste?

- What is taste?

- Where in my mouth am I actually tasting what I taste?

- How many different tastes can I identify?

- Can I distinguish the separate ingredients of the liquid? Where? What do they taste like?

- Can I taste the difference between the coffee and the cream? Can I taste the sugar? Where do I taste sugar? (Specifically, break it down.)

- What happens in my mouth as I begin to swallow? The various muscular activities? What does my tongue do? What does the head do?

- Where does the swallow begin?

- As I open my throat to receive the liquid, what muscles come into play?

- What do I feel when the liquid begins to run down into my throat?

Once you've done the exercise to the swallowing of the liquid, you must replace the cup on the table. This is still part of the exercise, because it is essential to keep the reality going to its logical conclusion. The cup cannot vanish in thin air. As you go through this final section of the exercise, continue asking sensory questions in the order in which they present themselves down to the final sounds of the cup hitting the table.

When you have spent many hours working with and without the object and breaking it down into small areas of exploration, then you should do the entire exercise straight through without referring back to the real object. Re-create it totally from your sensory memory. Not only is this the logical progression from sense memory but, when working in a play or a film, you must be able to create your choice, totally, without the presence of the real object.

The beauty of sense memory is that you have very few limitations. You can practice it anywhere, at any time and it takes no special equipment. You can work for heat in a chilly room. You can make music in deadly silence. You can create beautiful things on ugliness. The world is at the command of your imagination through the magic of your five doors of perception.

JELLYBEAN:

Sense Memory
Won't Work For You
Unless You Work For It.

ABOUT THE SENSE MEMORY EXERCISE

Two of the most important purposes of sense memory are your instrumental development—the training of your senses to be alive and responsive—and the development of your ability to create whatever realities you need to make you feel what the character feels. Sense memory will not pay off, however, unless you practice it daily over a period of time and make it a part of your life. If you really commit yourself to it you will find it to be a backbone tool for you which ultimately will elicit unconscious organic responses of astounding dimension.

Ask as many questions as you need in order to re-create the object. As you go along, you'll find your own rhythm, your own sensory needs. In the beginning, your instrument may require more questions than later on. In certain sensory areas you may have to ask many more questions than other areas, if that's a weaker sense for you. You might have to isolate one question and ask thirty related to it before the sense responds to that specific thing. Also, the nature of the object will often dictate its own investigation.

Choosing objects is a very important area. What is an object? For our purposes, an object can be anything, animate or inanimate, not just something you can see and pick up. An object can also be a sound, a smell, a temperature, a person, an animal, a time of year. At first, as we've said earlier, choose objects to eat or drink because they engage all five senses. As you progress, you'll find many reasons behind your choice of an object. To improve a sluggish tactile sense, you might spread fifty objects out on a table, all with a variety of textures, and close your eyes and investigate them all tactually. If your auditory sense needs work, you might blindfold yourself and navigate around the room just on the basis of sounds, or you might work with one object which is primarily sound-producing—a bell, a piece of music.

Choose objects which excite you, which interest you emotionally and sensorily, so that you don't get bored. Also choose objects with an awareness of their potential challenge to your senses. An object without any patterns or colors, something that has a bland, standard kind of shape doesn't really give your senses much of an adventure. Pick things with an eye to their complexity.

After you've been working with sense memory for a while, you'll choose objects quite individually to deal with your own sensory problems and you may be in the process of working with three or four different kinds of objects at the same time, each for different reasons. Sometimes you'll select something to work on just for clinical purposes to exercise your senses, as a pianist would stretch his fingers. You'll want to make yourself remain on that academic level to discipline your senses as an antidote to sloppiness. When you've been doing sense memory a long time, you tend to lapse into generalities and take things for granted. A purely academic workout gets you back on the track. But even though you start clinically, your exercises should all be adventures. Sense memory is something you should look forward to, anticipating it as a game you love to play, a sojourn into the unknown.

Following is a list of questions, a kind of checklist to help you understand and apply the Sense Memory Exercise. Don't use it like a pilot's checklist, literally checking out each item every time you take off. It's an overall map of elements, which eventually you will assimilate. Look it over before you begin and then put it aside. Soon the checklist will be internalized and become part of your work.

SENSE MEMORY CHECKLIST

- Am I asking enough questions?

- Am I asking the questions specifically? Do my senses understand the questions?

- Am I asking the right kinds of questions? Not intellectual ones, but the ones that appeal to my senses?

- Do my questions interest me? Do they affect me emotionally?

- Am I really concentrating on the object or am I just concentrating on concentrating?

- How do I feel? (Personal Inventory)

- Are my questions coming in logical sequence or are they violating the chronological order?

- Am I asking inventive, imaginative questions?

- Am I using my time well, allowing enough time to encourage my senses to answer, giving them enough time to respond?

- Do I have any tension? If so, where is it? Am I including it? And how can I alleviate it?

- Am I doing it for me?

- Am I getting a sense of the object? Do I really feel it, smell it, taste it or am I kidding myself?

- Am I being too precious or teensy-weensy? Am I being pedantic and specifying what is already specific?

- Am I unpredictable? Am I surprising myself?

- Am I tricking myself now and then?

- What does the object remind me of or suggest to me?

- Am I including everything that's going on, my thoughts, my feelings and distractions, and am I expressing these with the exercise?

- Am I letting the object suggest its own exploration?

- How can I have more fun and make it more of an adventure?

- Am I letting the exercise kick off thoughts and impulses that take me on a trip and am I allowing myself to go with that, without letting these digressions become endless?

- Am I really working sensorily or just suggestively?

- Do I allow myself to start with any sense or am I dependent on the same one?

- Have I located the object in space?

- Am I asking supportive questions in each category?

- Am I using the stronger senses to encourage the weaker ones?

- Am I asking hundreds, thousands of questions?

- Am I finding my sensory triggers?

- Do I let myself walk away for a while when it becomes too tedious?

MARATHON: SENSE MEMORY ROUND

The scene: A Marathon, January 12, 1972. A marathon acting session occurs every few months and is attended by a group of fifteen or twenty of my students who want to work at their craft intensively for twenty-four hours straight. At the moment the group is sitting in a circle doing an exercise called *The Sense Memory Round.* Each actor is working with his own inanimate object. One at a time, each actor asks a group of sensory questions out loud about his object and the other actors in the Round respond sensorily to those questions in relation to their own objects. After five or ten questions, I call on the next person to continue, but I don't go "around the circle" in order, because I've found that actors build up tension knowing when their turn is coming. The next person picks up where the last one left off and goes on in any direction from there.

Corinne: (Working with a small china statue) Where is it light and where is it dark on the object?

Eric: Not a good question to start that category, because you're drawing a conclusion by calling it light and dark instead of making your senses work.

Corinne: How does light affect the object?

Eric: Better. Much better.

Corinne: Which part of the object is exposed directly to the light?

A group of actors doing a "Sense Memory" round at a marathon.

Eric:	Good. That kind of question encourages your visual sense to investigate rather than accept a conclusion. Okay, Norman?
Norman:	(Working with a paperweight) I'm experiencing the weight.
Eric:	No. Ask a question about the weight.
Norman:	(A silence) I'm asking myself the question.
Eric:	Ask it out loud.
Norman:	What is weight? What does it feel like when it touches my palm? Extending from the back of my hand.
Eric:	That's a whole book you've asked. I don't understand the question. It's too fast, it's too widespread a question. It's not specific enough. Too general. Do you know what I mean by too general?
Norman:	No, I don't know what that means.
Eric:	All right, here's a specific question about the weight. "How does the weight of the object affect my hand in terms of the downward pressure I feel? Exactly where in my hand do I feel that downward pressure?" Norman, don't shake the object back and forth. Just keep it still in your hand and ask a question.
Norman:	How does it feel in my palm? Where are the points of. . .
Eric:	Before you pile on another question, give your palm a chance to respond.
Norman:	(After a pause) Where are the points of contact?
Eric:	Good.
Norman:	Where is it hard and soft?
Eric:	No, no, hard and soft are answers. They're conclusions. The texture, the resiliency, the mass, the resistance of the object—those are the areas you ask questions in. If

you use a word like *texture,* then your senses *must* supply the answers. Now slow it down, Norman. Go on.

Norman: Where is the air space between the points of contact?

Eric: Good. Very good. That's much more specific. Do you feel any responses to that? (Norman nods yes.) Cindy?

Cindy: (Working with an orange) How does the object feel on my fingers?

Eric: Finger first, then fingers. You're doing too much too fast, Cindy.

Cindy: Where do I feel the object on each finger?

Eric: Good. Take the time to answer with each finger.

Cindy: What are the differences in what each finger feels?

Eric: Good. I'd like you to pursue that. Leave the Round awhile and work over in that corner. Guy?

Guy: What is the temperature? (Pause) Where do I feel it? (Pause) What is the difference between the temperature of the object and the temperature of my hand?

Eric: Good questions. Good usage of time, Guy. John?

John: (He's working with an ashtray full of cigarette butts and an orange peel. He asks three or four questions in the area of temperature, picking up where Guy left off, then goes to the olfactory sense.) What do I smell? (Pause) How many odors am I aware of around me? (Pause) What's the strongest smell? (Pause) Can I smell the object from here? (The ashtray is on the rug about three feet below him.) As I bring my head toward the object, when does the odor increase? (Pause) As I lift the object, how close . . .

Eric: Wait a minute, John. You were doing great until then, but now you're violating the logical order of the reality. Something has to take place before you lift the object. Right?

103

John:	Oh, yeah, Eric. I was just concentrating on the olfactory.
Eric:	Do it chronologically, John, because I don't want you to violate everyone else's reality.
John:	Okay. How much pressure must I apply in my fingers so that I can grasp the object?
Eric:	Good.
John:	Where is the muscular tension in each finger? (John is an experienced student and gives himself enough time between each question.) In the hand? Wrist? Up the arm? How far up the arm before I feel any muscular tension? What does the resistance from the object feel like?
Eric:	Pamela, why are you crying?
Pamela:	I'm working for my dog. I loved him and he's dead.
Eric:	Pam, I don't want you to work for your dog. Everybody's working on inanimate objects today for a purpose. Inanimate objects are much easier to work with because they're constant, they stay the same. Animate objects are always changing, moving, blinking, breathing, going away, coming back, and all these things must be dealt with when you're working with animate objects. To work on a living thing—a person, an animal, you must have a greater degree of sensory sophistication and facility. That's not to say I discourage any of you from working on a person or an animal at any stage of your training, but be aware that you cannot approach it as an unchanging object. For today, in this Sensory Round, I want us to stick with inanimate objects.
Pamela:	Eric, I'm really *feeling* something right now! Why are you stopping me?
Eric:	I've no desire to stop you from feeling what you're feeling. But tell me, how did you get to that?
Pamela:	(Angry and sobbing) Well, I remembered this dog I used to have and I pictured her lying in front of me

with blood all over her and I remembered how I felt when she was run over.

Eric: Pam, I don't disbelieve your feelings, but as your teacher I feel responsible for your process. Your process was intellectual and suggestive and the emotional response from that kind of work is not dependable because it's retrospective.

Pamela: What do you mean, Eric? It worked for me.

Eric: Yes, but would it work for eight performances a week? Or will it evaporate on you because it isn't coming from a solid reality? Now, Pam, don't get me wrong. I don't mean for a moment that if something works for you, if something stimulates in you an organic, three-dimensional response and does it consistently—even if you say one word to yourself and it happens to you every time—I don't argue with that. And I'm saying this to all of you. Whatever works for you WORKS. Go with that, if it works consistently. You don't have to go through the sensory process, you don't have to go through any process, if you've got something that is truly real for you. Talent is talent. I never negate talent.

But Pam, what I saw you do, the reason I stopped you—now this is really important for you to understand—what I saw was something I call theatrical hysteria. You were crying and sobbing and lying on the carpet and talking about your dog, but it was coming out of tension and anxiety and your obligation to succeed and impress. I don't mean show off, but to be good as an actress. We all want to be good. That passes for real emotion on television and in the theatre and you're very good at that, Pam, but I stopped you because I don't want you to settle for that. It's conventional. It's shallow and predictable. I want you to be able to achieve a depth of meaning, an organic reality, a three-dimensional, unpredictable reality that comes out of a real choice. I believe you're capable of doing that. For now you are going to have to let go of something that you can do to reach for something that you can't yet do, but something that will be infinitely more exciting for your work. I understand how terrifying it is to let go and seemingly have nothing for a while, but

Pam, I'm urging you to do it, because the rewards will be phenomenal.

Pamela: What rewards, Eric? I'm so confused. I don't know where to go. I don't understand what any of this has to do with my dog.

Eric: Okay, listen. I had a dog. The dog's name was Holly. The dog was about so big and kind of tan, whatever. Okay. Holly died. I feel sad that Holly died. However, before she died a lot of years passed. There were a lot of feelings I had about Holly and if I want to re-create that relationship and feel those things I felt toward the dog and even some of the unconscious things I felt toward her, I must be capable of creating that animal here in front of me as that animal existed when it was alive. You follow me so far?

Pamela: I think so.

Eric: Okay. Now, in order to do that I must have a process of *sensory* memory so that I can create that animal in *total,* not just when she died with blood all over her, but hear her, feel her, see her and if I wanted to, taste her. Now this is not an intellectual process. I do not *think* about how Holly was when she sat there. I do not *picture* her, because that's just suggesting that the whole object is there instantly, without creating the component parts, which will make it fully real to me. I do not *remember* the sounds and smells in my head, because my brain does not have a nose. It doesn't have ears. My nose is my nose, my ears are my ears and those are the places I smell and hear. If all I do is *remember* how I felt about Holly, the memory of that feeling will not restimulate that feeling at all, only an intellectual, retrospective shadow of that feeling. I can remember that I felt sad and in doing so I might again feel sad about being sad.

However, if I want to have a three-dimensional rela- tionship to my dog, here and now, even to my dog being dead, I must first re-create my dog so that I can really relate to her. I must create her so that I can see her, smell her, hear her, feel her, taste her. I might even laugh. I might play with the dog. I might tickle the dog. The dog might bite my arm. The dog might run away from me. The dog must exist for me here and now. If the dog exists and I'm responding to it in terms of its reality, I can then work for the dog being dead. At that point I will respond to the dog's death totally, very dimensionally, honestly—as if it were happening here and now, because in fact it *is*.

Now, to be able to do that, I have to know, one, how my senses function and, two, how to make them aware and receptive and, three, the technical process of making them do my bidding and work for me and, four, I have to practice them. If I tell you how to do this tonight, you cannot come back tomorrow night and create your dog. Not tomorrow. Maybe after a lot of tomorrows. We're at the very first step in the creative process here and I'm going to forget about Holly for now because Holly is a very complicated living object that constantly changes. What I'm doing now with this inanimate object, this apple, this pencil, is I'm training my senses to sense memorize it with the purpose of re-creating this object's existence when it does not exist anymore. In doing so, I can later create Holly and my mother and my father and my uncle and all those people and objects that affected me deeply.

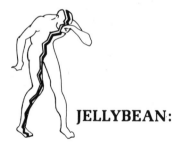 **JELLYBEAN:**

If Both Hands Are Full Of Fool's Gold How Can You Pick Up The Real Gold?

Sense memory should become a part of your way of life. Daily sit-down practice is only one aspect of it, although an important one, because you could practice it every day and even be quite facile in it, but not have it be a part of your life. Sense memory must belong to your philosophy. It's an integral part of your craft and your craft is more than a way of working. It's a way of living. Sensory work must profoundly influence the way you relate to things and perceive them. It's a continual process of looking and feeling and assimilating, breaking up the sensory component parts of objects that you can use later, and making on-the-spot discoveries of things that affect you. It should be happening with you always—riding on a bus, in a car, on a date with your lover, eating dinner, at a party. Wherever you are and whatever you're going through, you are constantly identifying the sensory elements and understanding how they affect you so that you can re-create those things right now or tomorrow or next month. You are cataloguing your life's experiences for future use on stage and you are also opening your instrument, each day expanding yourself to be more available to many more things.

Even though the process begins consciously at a point where you have to remind yourself to ask questions about what's going on around you, ultimately it becomes automatic. You take a mountain walk and hardly realize that you're listening for different sounds and collecting the various outdoor odors. Actors often complain, "I can't remember anything below the age of ten and even the stuff I remember, I can't recall how they smelled or tasted." Starting from today forward, take inventories of yesterday and the day before and this habit will gradually open up your sensory memory of earlier times in your life, building your repertoire of choices. Your conscious exploration releases your unconscious reservoir, and all kinds of colors from your unconscious begin flowing into your work. *The unconscious is where your real talent lives.*

Your sensory quest should go on twenty-four hours a day (dreaming is sensory too!), every day of your life.

Greg Mulavey doing a "Self-Inventory" exercise.

FINDING YOUR BEST TIME
AND PLACE TO WORK

You should do at least forty-five minutes to an hour of sit-down daily practice on inanimate objects. Choose the best time for you, the time when you are least distracted, most comfortable and most excited about sensory exploration. The place can be anywhere. Find a place you enjoy.

Joan: I'm a day person and I like to go to bed early. But often I wake up early in the morning, two-thirty, five o'clock, with a vague sense of unfinished business, which I relieve with an hour or two of sensory work and then I go back to sleep again. I keep by my bedside a few of my current objects—a hollow-stemmed champagne glass, a stone, a small pine cone, perfume, cough drops, etc. My king-sized bed is a special place for me. Over the years it's become not only my sleep place, but also my office, my playground and my rehearsal hall. In fact, in a Pavlovian way my bed actually stimulates me to work (which sometimes messes up my sleeping schedule)! When I want to find a choice or try out a choice to see where it takes me, the first thing I do is get on my bed. It's my magic place.

Early morning is often a good time for me to work, because I'm just rested enough, but still tired enough not to care too much. I have a tendency to try too hard and push for results, but at two-thirty in the morning I'm grateful if I feel anything at all. My mind is still foggy, so I don't get over-complex. My sensory responses happen naturally and simply and that pleases me and makes me want to do more. Also at that time of day I feel particularly vulnerable and alone, hanging out in space while everyone else is sleeping. For that reason I use this time to work on meaningful choices too, besides the bedside objects, because my defenses are down, my skin is thinner, and everything affects me more quickly and deeply.

SENSORY EXPLORATION
AND EXPERIMENTATION

The following group of exercises deal with your development in the sensory world. All of them relate in one way or another to discovery, exploration and experimentation with yourself and the objects in the world around you. If sense memory becomes an adventure that you look forward to, then you will begin to experience the magic of this work and eventually take possession of a powerful tool in the creative process.

4. Sense Memory Looked Forward To

Sense Memory Looked Forward To is a device, a way of getting yourself to enjoy and therefore practice sense memory. There are many things people enjoy and look forward to doing—having your back massaged, sitting in a hot tub after a long day's work, sensual pleasures, listening to your favorite piece of music, a glass of good wine. Whatever you look forward to doing in real life can make an excellent Sense Memory Exercise and if you enjoy it, you'll be more likely to practice sense memory.

5. Feelies

A feelie is any object you can carry in your pocket or purse. A feelie is also a smellie, a tastie, a hearie and a seeie. I used to carry all kinds of feelies in my pockets. My pockets looked like a junk shop—little bottles of liquid sen-sen, pieces of fabric, small stones, a rabbit's foot, a perfumed sachet. Waiting around in offices, I'd take something out of my pocket and work on it. Sitting in a restaurant having coffee and watching the world go by I'd take three or four objects out and lay them on the table and alternate between them.

6. Sense Memory Workout

• Get familiar with an inanimate object.

• Work without it.

• Get familiar with an animate object, person, animal.

• Work without it.

• Get familiar with some physical part of your own self.

110

- Work without it.

- Get familiar with an external object or body contact; hat, cape.

- Work without it.

- Get familiar with a sound or smell.

- Work without it.

7.   What-Not Boxes

This is an exercise for blind sensory investigation. A little what-not box is something you can construct. It's about two feet by two feet, all sides enclosed except for a hole in one side just big enough to get your hand in. Have someone in your family or a friend fill it with small objects that appeal to all the senses, a wide variety of them. Then, without knowing what's in there, put your hand in and, just by feeling each object, try to decide what it looks like, what its true shape is, what color it might be, what it might smell like, what sound it would make if it dropped to the floor. Supply these imaginary answers sensorily just by the tactile clues. Then take the objects out of the box and really find out how they look, taste, sound and smell.

A big what-not box is your house or a room in it. With your eyes closed move around the room smelling, tasting, hearing and feeling everything. Sensorily identify and explore the objects that you are visually familiar with and be aware of your sensory responses to objects that your sight has taken for granted. When you look at a fabric, your bedspread or draperies, you really don't know how it feels or tastes or smells. But when you're blind and you feel it, it takes on a whole new life. You'll find all tastes and smells and sounds become more vivid.

8.   On-the-Spot Sense Memorizing

Every day you will experience many things. Pick a fleeting experience—a bus passes you and the fumes hit you in the face—a telephone ringing in another room—your first sip of cold beer on a hot day at the beach—and just after it's gone, try to re-create the sensations in a minute or two. Keep it simple. Don't try to re-create too much. Ask maybe ten to twenty questions. You can do this fifty times a day with fifty different things. This exercise allows you to work for the imaginary elements shortly after you experi-

ence the real elements. As you do it over a period of time you col-
lect more and more objects to be used in the future. And it dis-
obliges you from having to do a complete Sense Memory Exercise
every time you decide to practice.

9.   Kinesthetics

The kinesthetic sense, described in Chapter II, is your muscular
response to the presence or absence of objects around you. With
your eyes closed, walk around slowly and carefully and try to sense
the objects and people around you without touching anything. Use
your kinesthetic sense to determine distances and positions of objects. It's fun to do it in the park in a large, open space with another
actor who (with his eyes open) moves in and out of your kinesthetic
range. After a while you really begin to know where he is.

10.   Sense Memory Guessing Games

These games include all the senses. They're good to play with friends,
with actors at rehearsals, at parties, but you can also do them alone.
One version is a group sitting in a room with their eyes closed and
one person walks around tapping things, dropping things, making
sounds of all kinds, holding odoriferous objects under people's
noses for identification. Identification is the way you win and
when you think you have an answer you raise your hand and say
where the sound comes from and what materials are involved in
making that sound—metal, plastic, wood. The leader can pass around
a tray with three or four jars of different substances, such as honey,
cottage cheese, ketchup, sour cream. Each person sticks one finger
in and without smelling or tasting it, describes out loud the sensation. The results of this one are often hilarious. The solo version of
the exercise is also entertaining. Sitting in your house and listening
to the cars go by, try to identify the makes by their sounds. Open
the kitchen cupboard, close your eyes, and use your sense of smell
and touch to know whatever is in there. Invent your own versions
of these games.

11.   Get a Sense of Being Naked

Do this exercise fully clothed. Of course, to achieve success in it
you will have had to practice it with and without clothes, as you do
in all sense memorizing. It's delicious to do this exercise secretly
while at a party or a wedding, because it produces a startling effect
on your behavior. If you're really successful in creating a sense of
your own nudity, you'll experience all kinds of unpredictable things.

When people look down at you, you'll get embarrassed and turn away. You'll find yourself blushing or giggling or behaving in sensually provocative ways. It engages the overall use of your body and you should use your whole body frequently to remind yourself that sense memory is not just your hand on a cup or your nose to a lemon. These fun-producing exercises will encourage you to do sense memory all the time.

12. Re-create a Moment from Today

Pick a moment of today when something vivid happened. It doesn't have to be a strong emotional event. It can be something pleasant and warm—you had lunch with a friend, you bought something you liked. Isolate a sensory element of the experience and try to re-create it. You had lunch today with a friend you hadn't seen in a long time. You were in an open patio restaurant and you really enjoyed the nostalgic dialogue of things you shared in the past. Out of the complexity of this experience you might choose to work for one sensory element of the warm afternoon sun on your face while you and your friend were talking. Re-create how that felt on your face specifically, the direction of the sun, the degree of heat, the difference in what you felt in each part of your face, etc. By doing just that, there's a strong possibility that you might re-experience some of the feelings you had that afternoon. And maybe you won't. Working for that element is enough.

13. Animate an Inanimate Object

This is more of a game than it is a Sense Memory Exercise, but it involves the senses and it's fun. It also stimulates your imagination. Take an inanimate object—a chair, a pencil, a typewriter—and endow it with a personality as sensorily as possible. Try to create its voice and really hear it. Give it movement, rhythm, visual activities such as crossing the room. Have an imaginary conversation with the object. Do it with all kinds of objects, anywhere and at any time.

14. The Desert Exercise

This is a marvelous Sense Memory Exercise. When done with a group of people, it can also be an improvisation. You're stranded in the desert and the point is to create all the elements of exposure, exhaustion, thirst, heat, the vastness of your isolation. Begin with one element—for instance, the heat. Start by making the room you're in hotter than it is. Then you might go to creating the desert around you visually, locating where the sun is. These elements support your working for heat. It may take you two weeks of doing the exercise to work up a sweat. Then go on, progressively adding one element at a time of the total reality. If you're successful, the heat itself may stimulate thirst. It's an excellent sensory workout and the rewards are very satisfying. The Desert Exercise is not recommended for people who are just beginning to do the work of sense memory.

WORKING WITH MEANINGFUL OBJECTS

In the application of sense memory to acting, your first step is to go from clinical practice with inanimate objects to objects which are meaningful to you. A *meaningful object* is anything that evokes an emotional response in you no matter how slight. In your sensory exploration you've undoubtedly come upon objects that have some kind of emotional impact on you. Now work on these meaningful objects deliberately, besides your apples and oranges, and form the habit of affecting yourself emotionally through the sense memory process. At this point you are not concerned with the emotional needs of a piece of dramatic material. Don't burden yourself yet with this obligation. As you become skilled at affecting yourself emotionally through sense memory, you should begin then to deal with dramatic material. After working with many meaningful objects you will know what kinds of things sound good, but don't affect you, as compared to the objects that really touch you.

Here are some suggestions of meaningful objects. Hopefully they will stimulate other ideas.

- Photographs

- Childhood toys

- A family pet

- High school yearbook

- Love letters

- Pressed flowers

- Your children

- Theatrical reviews

114

- A piece of jewelry

- Any of your bedrooms as you grew up

- A piece of meaningful music

- Any meaningful place in your life (army barracks, kindergarten, summer camp)

- Your mother

- Your father

- Your wife, husband, lover

OBLIGATION AND CHOICE

It is necessary now to define *obligation* and *choice* and how they relate to sense memory.

An *obligation* is that which exists in the scene that indicates to you what the character feels. That becomes what *you* want to feel. For instance, the character in the scene feels despondent, alone, without goal direction, suicidal. Those are your *obligations* in the scene. Those are all the things that you want to feel.

A *choice* is the object you choose to make you feel what the character feels. *Sense memory is the way you create the choice.* Your choice is the stimulus you will use sensorily to create the kind of behavior and emotional life you want in the scene. Your choice might be to re-create a simple piece of music, a certain melody that makes you feel despondent and alone. A choice can be almost anything. A place, a time and a place, a piece of furniture, a person, an aroma, a sound, the kinesthetic feeling of the presence of someone outside the door or in back of you, a piece of clothing, an external sense of being something other than what you are, such as an object or an animal or another person. A choice can be anything that works for you. You choose it in the hopes of stimulating not only a single identifiable emotion, but also a complicated emotional life.

Some choices need not be translated sensorily, because the approach to creating the object is clear. You're working for a certain offensive odor, because your obligation is to feel nauseous. It's a clear Sense Memory Exercise. Or you're working for an award you

Anna Ivara doing a "Dump" exercise

won, a gold statuette, because it makes you feel accomplished and proud. These are both simple objects and all you do to create them is ask the questions and answer them with your senses.

But some choices require sensory translation before you can begin the process of creating them. For instance, if you want to restimulate the hurt you felt when a certain person criticized you over the telephone, where would you begin? Ask yourself what exactly it was that made you feel hurt. Your answer will be what that person said to you over the phone. Since you cannot create that voice out of mid-air, you start by sensorily creating the phone in your hand and at your ear. Then once you have a sense of the telephone, you create the voice, the sound of it, the pitch, the rhythm, the peculiarities of it. Finally you create the words themselves which hurt you. You will know when you have to translate a choice sensorily, simply because reality dictates its own order. If your starting point on a choice is obvious to you, then start. If you don't know where to start, you will have to translate that choice sensorily before creating it. The translation is just a device which tells you where to start and how to work for your choice.

The trip from your practice training with coffee cups and inanimate objects to the fulfilling of a strong emotional obligation, such as a character about to commit suicide, is a long trip. It begins with your first sit-down sensory exercise. Your ability to create a cup of coffee so that you can really see it, feel it, taste it, smell it, hear it is the same ability that you must have to create the objects necessary to make you feel suicidal. That's the connection between coffee cups and suicide.

USING SENSE MEMORY
IN SCENE WORK

Before finishing this chapter, we want to give you an example of how *obligation, choice,* and the *sensory approach* fit together in a scene. The following is a taped excerpt from a class demonstration. For the last several weeks, Lori and Allen have been working on a scene adapted from Hemingway's short story "The Hills Are Like White Elephants." I'm using the circumstances of this material to illustrate some points to the class . . .

Eric: If I were doing a scene with Lori and we were lovers and
         we'd been living together for a long time and she's preg-

117

nant and I feel guilty about it and yet I love her and I don't want her to have the baby—those are the realities and obligations in the material. Okay, the first thing I must feel is love for her, because unless I care about her I can't feel guilty or have any of those conflicts. So I'll start simply with the obligation to love her. And before deciding on what to work for, I'll start with what exists.

How do I feel about Lori? I feel warm and affectionate about her. I like her. But that isn't enough to fulfill the obligation. So I need a choice. Instead of creating things in Lori I love, knowing me and my needs, it would be easier to love someone if I could see they loved me. So I'll work to create love for me from Lori. I might see a love in her eyes, a warmth, an attraction for me, a vulnerability toward me, because I created it there. I create that look in Lori's eyes by asking questions sensorily: "Where do I see that warmth in Lori's eyes?" First in the left eye. Then I ask the question of the right eye. What happens to her eyes when she smiles? What actually is love when it manifests itself in an eye? It really isn't in the eye itself. It's all around the eye—the welling up of tears, the wrinkles around the eye, the light changes. Now if I pursue this investigation, asking many more questions, and not just visual ones, I might have the beginning of a relationship of loving Lori

One obligation, one choice, one sensory approach.

and caring about her very much. I'm not dealing with any of the other obligations yet, the guilt and the discomfort, just the love. And I'm working with her eyes as my choice, hoping it will do for me what I want it to do. It may not. I may sit here and at the end of that rehearsal time I may say, "Hey, you know I liked it, Lori, but I don't feel the things I want to feel." Then I may have to boost my choice, add to it or go for another choice altogether. And I'm still working for that one element of caring for her, loving her. *One obligation, one choice, one sensory approach.*

Now while I'm working for my choice in relation to Lori, Lori exists and anything Lori does will affect me, hopefully, because I'm open to her. This is the area where most actors go down the tubes, because they want to act, they want to behave, they want to feel what the author tells them to feel. All I feel is what Lori makes me feel and what my choice makes me feel. I'm going to say the lines and I'm going to ask the sensory questions in between and include all the life that's going on in me. That's what I express, the sum total of the questions and their responses and all the life that's going on. In rehearsal you work for your choice at the cost of the material until you find out if that choice, fully explored, will complement the material or not.

THE REWARDS OF SENSE MEMORY

In order to create an object that does not exist, it may take you seven hundred questions before you get the beginnings of a sense of it. After you become a master craftsman, through years of hard work and application, instead of saying in the Second Act transition, "I will work for my grandmother and I'll ask how high does she stand in the doorway, how much of the door does she take up, what color is her hair, etc.," you will have become so sensorily alive and knowing of your instrument that when you pick up your script and say, "Okay, in the Second Act I'm going to work for my grandmother," all you'll do is say, "Grandma!" and it'll all be there. You'll get the same full, complete response from the mere suggestion of the choice that you would have gotten in your first year after asking four hundred questions. Ultimately your instrument becomes so pure and so totally responsive that it asks and answers the questions at the same time. The craft then is no longer a craft, because you have become the totality of it.

119

Libby Thompson learning to work for a "Sense Memory Choice", creating cold, heat or some other physical sensation.

All of your creativity comes from the bedrock of YOU.

Chapter
4

PREPARATION

"METHINKS I HEAR A CANNON"

Acting is ninety-five per cent preparation. If you are ready to act, then you can.

The Scene: An agent's office in New York City. An actor is sitting in the waiting room reading the trades. In the inner office the agent is talking on the phone, "No, . . . I don't handle any last-minute one-line actors . . . I don't know *any* actors who'd take one line up at Stratford tonight even if it *is* Shakespeare!"

At this point, the actor rushes in from the waiting room and whispers desperately, "I'll take it! I'll take it!" The agent wraps up the deal and that same afternoon the actor finds himself on a train to Stratford. Like Rodin's *Thinker*, his head is resting in his hand, his elbow propped on the windowsill. He looks deeply into the passing scenery without seeing. His lips move, silently repeating his one line of dialogue. "Methinks I hear a cannon . . . Methinks I hear a cannon . . . "

At the same time, he ponders what to use for his preparation. He knows he should start with relaxation, but he must also find some choices for his role, because he's a Method actor and wouldn't dream of going on stage unprepared. "I think I'll use a migraine headache," he decides, "because migraine headaches make me feel rotten. I want to get that going and then I'll work for a bad lung, because that will center me, make me feel something's really going on inside. Methinks I hear a cannon . . . Methinks I hear a cannon . . . Now I need one more thing to give me the spine of the character. I'll work for my father. I hated my father. That'll give me a real emotional force . . . Methinks I hear a cannon . . . Methinks I hear a cannon . . . "

He arrives at the theatre. They suit him in armor and give him a spear. An hour before curtain time he is pacing backstage, working on his preparation and repeating his one line. They give him the five-minute warning and tell him where to stand. He takes his position and continues his diligent preparing. The curtain goes up. There is a loud cannon blast. He recoils and exclaims, "WHAT THE HELL WAS THAT?"

MISUNDERSTANDING PREPARATION

This is a classic Method joke known to almost everyone. It illustrates several important problems related to people's misconception of "The Method." An actor who doesn't understand either the purposes or the uses of preparation makes preparation a thing unto itself. This is how "The Method" got its bad reputation. The Cannon joke shows how an actor can get so involved in extraneous and confused preparation that the process hinders rather than helps.

What is preparation? Preparation is the work you do to get you to the point where you can do your work. Many actors think that is a specific thing you do to get to a specific state, but that is only one kind. There are numerous kinds—lifelong preparations for your own growth as an artist, instrumental preparations, daily practice, preparations for a relationship to another person in a play, preparations to change your ego-state and many other kinds. An actor should be familiar with all forms of readiness besides the readiness to say the lines.

I used to think that preparation was only a state that you had to achieve so that you could act. Certainly that's a creative and organic form of preparation, but if that's the only kind you ever learn, then you are limited to that one state of readiness. Where do you go from there? AN ACTOR PREPARES—to do what? One preparation you use may only lead to the next level of preparation. For example, I walk into a theatre to rehearse a play and I'm tense that day and insulated and I'm not sensorily alive and I've had a bad day and I'm protecting myself. So I might begin with a relaxation exercise. Then I'd sensitize and do a Personal Inventory, and then maybe a couple of Vulnerability exercises. Hopefully, by then I'd feel open and ready to work. The scene obligates me to be concerned, compassionate and unable to help the situation. When I walked into the theatre, I couldn't have cared less about anyone. After these initial preparations, I may still not be compassionate, but I'm ready now to do a second kind of preparation, which is to work for choices that might take me to feeling what the character feels. My first level of preparation was preparation to prepare.

These two kinds of preparation depend entirely on your daily practice preparations. Are you practicing daily your relaxation, Sensitizing, Personal Inventory and Sense Memory so that when you try to use them, you can? All of this is based on the philosophy of BEING. If you don't regularly practice getting to the reality of what is going on in you, then when you start to work, you are not functioning from your true origin. The daily practice of BEING is your instrumental preparation. So far we've described four kinds of preparation that are implicit just by the actor walking into the theatre for a rehearsal. The nature of your preparation will always be determined by what you need at that moment.

The Cannon story illustrates how an actor often deludes himself into believing that the work he's doing is helping him, when actually that work is only adding to his burden and preventing him from seeing the simplest truths and responding to what he sees and hears. Had the Cannon actor simply listened, he would have heard the cannon and responded honestly to that. Instead he had a predetermined concept of the character as being much more complicated than was written and his preparation, rather than leading him to a state of BEING, only fortified his cerebral complexity, taking him farther and farther away from his real obligations.

Many so-called Method actors pay lip service to the craft while their preparations run parallel to what they've already decided to do and do not at all influence their resultant behavior. They'd act the same with or without preparation. That is why many actors, reputed to be Method-trained, turn out performances which are mannered and cliché.

You must always start first with getting to what is—here and now— right or wrong for that role. Only in a state of BEING can you really know what you need at that moment and then be able to select the right preparations. If you do not start with the real truth, your own truth, you cannot service the truths in the material. Only from a state of BEING can you hope to make a connection with your unconscious life.

BEGIN BY *BEING*

The bedrock of YOU—all of your creativity comes from that. BEING becomes a part of your daily lifetime preparation. BEING is the totality of everything you are, including everything you feel and the expression of that. The following group of exercises relate to BEING and, since that is the first step in the process of preparation, you should most often start there.

1. One-Person *BEING*

We've already described this exercise in Chapter 1, page 25. Find your own ways to practice it daily.

2. Two-People *BEING*

Described in Chapter II, page 76. The exercise can best be used as a daily preparation at those times when you are working on a scene with another actor and you meet periodically for rehearsals.

3. Personal Inventories

Described in Chapter I, page 25, and Chapter I, page 27. Practice it daily as often as you can. Besides asking yourself "How Do I Feel and What Do I Want," put special emphasis on "Am I Expressing What I Feel and If Not, Why Not and What Can I Do About It?" This last group of questions particularly relates to the obstacles that keep you from expression.

4. The *BEING* Workout

This exercise is done with a series of changing partners in a group setting, either an acting class or a rehearsal group. You can also adapt it for your daily BEING practice by doing it encounter-style with each person you meet, or whenever your common sense tells you it's applicable.

Start by relating to your partner on a here-and-now basis, acknowledging all the distractions that keep you from relating, including your self-consciousness and your concerns outside the relationship. Also deal with *obstacles* between you and the other person that keep you from BEING with that person, such as your fear, your worry about doing the right thing, social obligation, sexual attraction, hostility, unsaid feelings, repulsion, your impression that the other person expects something from you, lack of interest in the other person, etc. Unless these things are acknowledged and expressed audibly or semi-audibly, they will prevent you from BEING comfortable and organic in your relationship to that person.

Repeat the exercise with each one of your changing partners. Each person will present a different set of obstacles, some less than others. Repetition of the BEING workout builds the habit of eliminating the obstacles that keep you from being yourself with anyone. The goal is to accept the life that is, no matter what it is, and to become more comfortable with uncomfortable feelings. *Once you have acknowledged and expressed the obstacles to BEING, then you can BE.*

There's a story about an old-school, Russian-Jewish actor who visits his old friend, an author, and says to him, "I don't know. You are a writer and you are sitting down and you are typing something, finishing a script, looking at the script. You are working, you got something to look at. A painter, he paints a picture, he sees his picture. *I* am working and I am finished and all I have is spit on the mirror."

Writers write, painters paint, dancers dance, but actors sit and drink coffee. Or they stay in their rooms, like the wistful old man in the story, practicing the wrong things and ending up with nothing but spit on the mirror. There are many reasons why actors don't commit themselves to preparation as a way of life, to a daily regimen of practice. One reason is a lack of knowledge about what to practice. Acting teachers say, "Go out and observe." Observe what? How? And how do you use it? Ignorance of what to work on leads to the avoidance of work altogether.

Other actors, diligent and dedicated but without solid knowledge of their craft, practice things that are not helpful to their growth. Also the lack of a tangible product deters many an actor from homework, as the old man complains in the story. At the end of a practice session, you cannot lay your hands on your work, on a painting or a statue or a novel. The loneliness of daily practice is all the more poignant when there seem to be no tangible rewards.

But there *are* rewards. Each day you build a bank account of skills with which you can create realities and when you get on stage, you have a great deal more than just spit on the mirror. There isn't a serious artist in the world who doesn't spend every day working at his art. Somerset Maugham used to sit down at nine o'clock every morning to write and he'd write his name over and over again until an idea came to him. He did this for discipline.

JELLYBEAN:

Desert Your Art For One Day And It Will Desert You For Three

DAILY PRACTICE

Here are some things you should do every day. You should deal every day with some aspect of your ability to relax. You should Sensitize more than once a day. Do Personal Inventories as often as you can fit them into your daily activities. Observation exercises such as Observe, Wonder and Perceive, the Farmer's Market, etc. Sense Memory daily, with and without objects. All kinds of BEING exercises. Self Inventories to build up your stockpile of choices. These exercises and many others that appear in this book should be practiced daily by every actor.

Then, of course, as you learn to know your individual needs, you will also use instrumental exercises daily to overcome those specific problems.

All the exercises in this chapter can be practiced daily depending on your individual needs. And all of them lead ultimately to the fulfillment of dramatic material as well as expanding your growth as a person.

There are three major categories of preparation and all the exercises in this chapter fall into one or more of these categories.

1. **Instrumental Preparations**

    These are all the exercises related to *you,* to your living and acting problems. You are your instrument. You may have problems relating to tension, fear, inhibition or insulation. Your preparations in this category will focus on alleviating these and other instrumental problems. The preparations you do in this area analogous to the scales a concert pianist practices. You exercise to open your instrument, dealing with the obstacles that get in the way of being free and ready to work.

2. Preparations for Relating to People, Objects and Places

These are the exercises that enable you to relate to people outside of yourself and to objects and to your physical environments. Since living and acting are inseparable, you practice in your day-to-day relationships so that you become more observant, sensitized, affectable and responsive to external stimulation. As you are more vulnerable to people, objects and places, you will have more success in using these elements as choices in dramatic material.

3. Preparations for Doing the Role

These are the things that get you ready to do the part, the role, the scene, to fulfill the emotional obligations of the material.

These three categories often depend on one another. It would be impossible to prepare to do the scene if you were not instrumentally ready to work. In the scene you're doing, you might have a lot of difficulty relating to the other character if you have not prepared to relate. Also, the following exercises often overlap each other from one category to the next. You can use many of them for many purposes. For instance, a Vulnerability exercise is a part of your instrumental preparation, but you could, at times, use it specifically to fulfill an emotional obligation in a role or a scene. The three categories are only to make clear to you the reasons why you're doing whatever it is you're doing.

It is important to observe and understand all kinds of human behavior.

I. INSTRUMENTAL PREPARATIONS

A. Preparations for Awareness

Awareness is an ongoing process, a daily conditioning. Preparations for elevating your awareness should become a way of life. The exercises here are designed to make you more aware. As you go along, you should discover and invent more of your own.

5. The Cluster of Four

For a number of years, I've been starting my classes every week with The Cluster of Four, because I've found it's an ideally balanced group of exercises to begin with. The Cluster consists of relaxation (Logey, Tense and Relax, Deep Breathing, Rag Doll, etc.), Sensitizing, Personal Inventory, and What Do I Want as part of the Personal Inventory. Chapter II contains full descriptions of all of these. It's important to say that the sequence of The Cluster was not arrived at by accident, but by trial and error and success. First of all, you deal with your physical tension so that you can then Sensitize, raising your senses to higher levels of sensitivity. Then you go on to find out how you feel and what you want through Personal Inventory.

6. Super Consciousness

Start with an arbitrary decision to become super conscious, super aware of everything going on around you in all five sensory areas. You decide, "I'm now going to be super conscious. I'm going to hear every possible sound so that my ears can record the most obvious sounds down to the most subtle. I'm going to see, smell, taste, touch everything. I see all the fruit and papers on the table and I devour it through all my five senses, ingesting every detail like a sponge."

Do it for ten or fifteen minutes. It's a somewhat unnatural exercise in that your acute observations usurp a more natural moment-to-moment flow of life and you may not be able to relate to anyone while you're doing it, unless that person becomes the object of your Super Consciousness and then you will relate to him quite unnaturally. However, daily repetition of Super Consciousness automatically raises your level of awareness.

130

7. Farmer's Market

In Chapter II this exercise is explained thoroughly. We remind you here that it applies to your instrumental preparation for awareness.

8. Observe, Wonder and Perceive

Also described in Chapter II. Actors are notoriously self-involved and narcissistic. This simple exercise is very difficult for many actors, because the habit of being aware and observant of some-one other than yourself often comes hard. But with regular prac-tice, Observe, Wonder and Perceive—as with all these exercises—transcends from a deliberate decision to becoming a part of your life.

DIALOGUE ON CRAFT

Eric: How many times have you heard me say, "The craft is designed to do away with itself"?

Joan: Many, many times. And I've experienced it, because in this last play I was in, I certainly wasn't taking notes on each of these processes during my performances, but in retro-spect when I came offstage I could define for you as on a road map many of these things that were going on auto-matically *while* I was tending to the play. Simultaneous habits. Personal Inventory was going on all the time in the lines and in between the lines. Sensory Awareness. Vul-nerability. My observation, wonderment, perception were constant. All of these exercises weren't exercises anymore. They were me.

Eric: As a result of conditioned responses through practice. Good point. Now to make the point very clear, the transi-tion from an exercise to a way of life relates to what I just said—the craft is designed to do away with itself. If you do these exercises often enough, repeatedly, in your day-to-day living, in your acting, in your rehearsals, in your life, they become a part of the moment-to-moment fabric of your BEING. They become *you.*

9. Sensory Inventory

We go into this exercise in full detail in Chapter II. Sensory Inventory is the investigation of all your senses and what makes them work, how they are affected by external stimuli. An important point—as you repeat the exercise day by day, your sensory acuity grows and more and more parts of each sense begin to function. So it's an endless investigation that stimulates an increasingly higher and higher level of sensory awareness.

10. Sense Memory

This exercise is one of the best kinds of stimulation for awareness. Do a Sense Memory Exercise every day of your life from fifteen minutes to three hours. Spend as much time as you can on it. Sensory training progressively heightens your accessibility, sensorily and emotionally. While you are practicing, encouraging your senses to respond to imaginary stimuli, you will be astonished at the steady expansion of your awareness.

11. Sensuality

This is a three-part exercise you can do either alone or in a group. I've found it to be effective following The Cluster of Four. The first part has to do with sensuality related to your own body. The second part is sensuality toward inanimate objects and the third part, which you would omit if you were doing it alone, is sensuality related to other people.

Start with the first part, touching yourself with your hands all over your body. Sensorily and sensually feel the shapes and contours of your body, your muscularity, the varying textures of your skin and clothing. Encourage your body to respond to the touch of your hands, besides being aware of what your hands are feeling, so that tactually you are responding on both ends. Allow your body to find its own sensual rhythm and movement as you explore it, tasting yourself, smelling yourself and hearing your sensual sounds. Help yourself to make sounds that come out of your feeling of sensuality and let the rhythmic movements of your body flow together with your sounds to create your own beat. Include your genital areas and any sexual response that is part of the sensuality. This first section of the exercise builds slowly until your entire body is involved and moving—your neck, your head, your shoulders, arms, wrists, ankles, knees, as well as the pelvis area.

Then you go to the second part, to objects. Sensually relate to the wall, the floor, the rug, the chair, any objects in the room, such as a purse or jacket or book or an ashtray. Expose all parts of your body to the object so that your entire body relates to it sensually. If it's a small object, move it around on your face, in and around your mouth, under your arms, your chest, your stomach, inside of your thighs to the bottoms of your feet. If it's the rug or the wall, make total contact, front and back, letting every contour of your body touch the wall and as in the first part of the exercise, stimulate a rhythmic movement, your own sensual beat, as you taste, smell, and listen to the friction of your body against the object.

Then you go to people. You might start by just touching each other's hands, or put your cheek up against a thigh or bury your face in someone's hair and smell it, taste it and let it tickle your skin. You might stand back to back and make rhythmic contact and sensually enjoy the sounds and movements. Encourage yourself to taste and smell and touch things that you might conventionally avoid, such as smelling someone's shoe or tasting a toe or chewing on the strap of a handbag or chair. Sometimes you do this with two people, sometimes three or four or six. Sometimes it culminates in a whole mound of people sensualizing with one another.

The exercise often stimulates a degree of sexuality, which is all right if you are using it as a preparation for sexuality. However, its main purpose is to increase your awareness and the sensory availability of your entire body. A variation of the exercise is called Primal Sensuality, which is done the same way except that you approach it from the beginning with a larger commitment to be more animal and primitive in both your movements and sounds. This variation serves to break down barriers more quickly.

There are endless exercises for awareness besides the ones suggested here. Any one of these could branch off into a whole group of exercises. As you work daily you will come upon many things that work for you particularly and these will grow into your own repertoire of awareness preparations.

B. Ego Preparations

As an actor at school I was known as "the brooding Dane," because I was so often depressed. For years, as I worked professionally, I seldom felt I had the right to be heard, the right to take the time to prepare when other people were waiting for me to start the reading,

"Take Your Due" exercise

the right to stop in the middle of a take and do it over. I did what most actors do: I did what I thought was expected of me at the cost of what I really had to offer.

It was not until I started teaching that I found ways to help myself as an actor, because as a teacher I could see objectively, while dealing with other actors, how important it was to isolate and define this whole area of the actor's ego and how it affects his work. There are good race horses that lose the race because they don't get out of the gates. As a teacher I noticed that very talented people, even the most talented people, often had difficulty getting out of their gates, getting beyond their depressions and insecurities, so that they could use their craft and function creatively. Once they started to act, their talent would sometimes carry them through, but it wasn't something they could count on. I saw that it was at this beginning point, this pre-starting point, where many actors would get stuck, and rather than find ways to help themselves, they'd panic and fake it, imposing behavior to meet the theatrical demands.

I observed that actors suffer from a variety of ego-ailments, insidious demons that whisper to them, "You're not good enough . . . Nobody wants you . . . You're too old . . . You're too young . . . You're not good-looking enough . . . You don't have enough talent . . . You never went to college . . . You're a fool to keep trying . . ." In the work we did in class, the whole concept of the actor's ego-state became more and more important as part of his instrumental preparation. I took some common sensical exercises and devised others, inventing some fortunate accidents that happened during scenes and during individual work and created an area which I call Ego Preparations.

There must be at least seventy-five exercises in this area alone, which we practice in class and which actors who've studied with me use in their professional work. All of the exercises help the actor to change his ego-state to a better ego-state in which he can feel like working and allow himself to succeed. The exercises have many different emphases to match whatever the ego-difficulty is at that moment. When you feel insecure about your ability to act, you can do an ego exercise affirming the solidity of your craft (Count Your Craftual Blessings). If you are ready to work, but you feel physically insecure, disgusted with how you look, there are exercises for raising your physical self-acceptance. If you feel negative and depressed, you can do any number of Positivity exercises. If you're afraid to be heard making large statements, you can choose from many kinds of large-commitment exercises to help yourself. The selection is limitless, depending on what you need.

Besides supporting your readiness to work, you can also use an ego exercise as a choice to fulfill the emotional obligations in a scene from a play. If you want to feel bad, but that night you're feeling good, you might reverse one of the Ego Preparations to bring yourself down. Or maybe you're feeling neutral, not depressed, but not excited either. You might first want to do an Ego Preparation to lift your state to something more alive and inspired so that you can then sink down into the required depression, but still have exciting impulses.

Ego Preparations are an integral part of your instrumental preparation, because without sufficient acceptance of yourself, you cannot reach your talent, no matter how much talent you have.

12. Get a Sense of What You Used to Be

This is a morale-building exercise. Often an actor will despair at how far he has to go down the road. "Look at how far I have to go!" This exercise says to him, "Look how far you've come!" He gets a perspective on his growth over the past three to five years.

There are two ways you can do it. First, you can simply remember how you were three to five years ago, how you related to people, how you handled certain situations, the acting jobs you had and how you approached your craft. You can either think about these things or talk about them to yourself or to a group. The second way is to do an affective memory exercise and truthfully re-experience yourself at that time. This way is more time-consuming and complicated, but it has the added benefit of giving you a kind of behavior that you could use in a script.

13. Take Your Due

Most effective done in a group or with another person. Express out loud in words and action all the positive things you feel you have coming to you. Ask for what you want from various people around you. "Joe, I want you to pay more attention to me. Sue, I want you to take me more seriously. I want you all to stop talking while I'm doing this exercise." Talk about areas in which you feel you've been misunderstood and you haven't received your due. "None of you know this, but I'm a terrific photographer and I paint well and some day I'm going to be recognized for the actor I am. Peter, you think I'm overly critical of you, but I really expect a lot of you because you're very talented and that's why I demand so much. I want all of you to know that I'm filled with love. I have a lot of love to give and I want you to be open to accept it."

As you do this exercise repeatedly, your trust grows. You gain confidence in your ability to make your own statement. Remember to make your statement physically as well, standing up to your full height, taking up your rightful space, allowing yourself to be flambuoyant in your gestures if you wish.

Of course, there are some actors who misinterpret any exercise. I had a student once, a husky young man named Mickey. Every time I gave him this exercise, he'd systematically tear up the theatre, flinging chairs from wall to wall, ripping pillows. He even fractured his hand once ramming it through a door. I finally decided to give my *theatre* its due and stopped asking him to do this exercise.

14. Sense of Worth

You can do it alone or in a group. The purpose is to put you in touch with your worthy accomplishments. People often tend to minimize or forget things which they've worked very hard to accomplish. Express all your abilities and successes and in so doing you will bring to the surface a sense of worth that you may not have started with.

15. Don't Care

Do it alone or in a group. You say, "I don't care about _____. I don't care that _____. I don't care for _____. I couldn't care less that _____." A sample: "I don't care what goes on in Washington. I don't care about trivial gossip. I don't care what Betty just said about Jean. I don't care if I'm not always understood. I used to care about that a lot, but I don't anymore. I don't care as much about being good as I used to. I don't care for a lot of people," etc.

This exercise allows you to clean house mentally and frees you from concerns so that you can relate to what you really *do* care about. Sometimes a conglomeration of concerns makes you feel oppressed and weighted down. Deliberate expurgation of these things you don't care about can lessen your load and put your ego in a different place so that you can work.

16. Positivity and Validation

There are two ways to approach the Positivity exercise. You start with whatever positive impulses you really feel and verbalize them. "I kind of like being here. It's a nice place. I like some of the people here. I feel physically good . . ." Build from there, looking for more and more positive things to get involved in. If that leads you to more and more positive feelings, good. If it doesn't, you can then begin to exaggerate, being arbitrarily positive, until you feel more positive.

The second approach is the way you start the exercise when you are feeling so negative that even the thought of being positive is impossible. You can then begin with the deliberate decision to exaggerate, even to lie. You make an arbitrary commitment to say only positive things about everything you see, hear, taste, smell and touch. "This is a *beautiful* theatre. I love the color of the walls. (The walls may be dung brown, but say it anyway.) All those beautiful people are out there, paying attention to me and sending me signals of love. I feel terrific. I feel overwhelmed with creativity," etc. Hopefully, you will connect at some point with the seeds of your buried positivity.

Validation is a variation of the Positivity exercise. You go around the room and express supportive, validating thoughts about each person. "Corinne, I think you're a very warm and giving person. I'm glad you're here. John, I love the way you're dressed tonight. Your concern with the way you look has really grown. Danny, you're super talented. Allen, your sense of truth is marvelous." In other words, you give out sincere compliments and by honestly validating others, you begin to feel better about yourself, thereby changing a negative ego-state to a positive one.

17. Fun Exercises

Stimulate your own sense of fun in any way that you can. Get up there and be a baggy pants clown. Imitate a rooster. Walk around like a chicken and cock-a-doodle-doo. Make funny faces and crazy sounds at everybody. Be as silly as you can, a "silly-dilly." Distort your body into ridiculous positions and talk gibberish to people in the room. If that doesn't make you feel better, nothing will.

18. Comparative Ego

Do this exercise silently so as not to alienate anyone. Find in each person around you the things that make you feel better off than he or she, whether it's physical, intellectual, emotional, financial, theatrical. You think to yourself things like, "I'm glad I have enough money so I don't have to scrounge for it the way Jane does . . ." "I'm better looking than Harry and I'm younger." "I've done much more work than most of these people." "Who here knows more than I do about acting?" Do the Comparative Ego until you feel better and you can do it anywhere, on a movie set, on the street, in a class, at a party.

19. Make Yourself Beautiful

This exercise deals with your physical self and you use the sensory process to create a greater sense of yourself. Start with what is, defining what you really feel good about, even if it's only one thing. Maybe you have a good bust. Parade it around. Relate to it with pride. Emphasize and magnify it, feeling your sense of power in that area. Strut around the room and intensify your somewhat positive feelings about yourself into extremely positive feelings, finding as many real things as possible.

The next step is imaginary. Sensorily endow yourself with imaginary attributes. Caress your face and endow it with satin skin, petal-soft. Surround yourself with delectable odors emanating from your body. Make yourself bigger where you want to be bigger and smaller where you want to be smaller. Look into a real or imaginary mirror and create a dazzling reflection with sparkle in your eyes and highlights in your hair.

20. Take-Over or Evangelist

This is a large-commitment type of exercise designed to excite yourself and others, to get your adrenalin going. It's excellent for passive people, for soft-spoken and shy actors and actresses, whose egos need a boost. You simply make a large commitment to "taking over" a group of people and like a circus barker you sell them anything from an idea to a health product to religion to smoke-colored glasses for looking at eclipses. Capture their attention and hold it through your own excitement. Lecture to them, preach, chant, become an evangelist, a revivalist. Even if the exercise feels uncomfortable at first and out of character for you, jump in and do it arbitrarily. In a short time you will be caught up in the momentum and it will carry you along. Your ego will become buoyant.

21.   Magic Pocket

A marvelous ego exercise, which depends on your imagination. You can do it through a simple suggestion or through sense memory. Imagine that in one of your pockets you have something magnificent. A contract to a studio for seven years with astronomically escalating salaries. A telegram saying that you've won the Academy Award. Keys to a Rolls Royce parked outside. A wallet that never runs out of money. A letter from someone you've always loved and don't see anymore, asking you to join that person on an ocean voyage. You have in your pocket anything you can imagine being there either in reality or symbolically. The magic aspect of the exercise is vital. You must encourage yourself to believe in the magic. Walk around with your hand in your pocket or patting the outside of it and allow the belief to grow until you feel totally in possession of the most important thing in your life.

22.   Yeah! Yeah!

"yeah . . . Yeah . . . YEah . . . YEAh! . . . YEAH! *YEAH!! YEAH!!!*" Starting small and building to a crescendo, you say the one word over and over, bigger and bigger until it becomes a gigantic shout from the soles of your feet to the top of your head. The force of that positivity will fill your whole being and excite everyone around you. The exercise makes you want to go out and push down walls.

23.   Feel and Affirm Self
(Superman and Superwoman)

Make physical contact with your body, touching your muscles, whether you're a man or a woman. Press, knead and pat those parts where you feel strong and encourage the strength to grow in those parts and circulate and course through the rest of you. Flex your muscles, strut, pose, stand erect, squeeze the muscles of your thighs as you stride along and with each step become aware of your external and internal strength. You can accompany your movements with sounds either verbal or non-verbal, in a simplistic way, such as, "I AM. I FEEL. I'M STRONG. I FEEL MY POWER." You will experience a growing affirmation of yourself.

Since you are one of a kind, unique unto yourself, your ego concerns will be individual and you will learn what you need in this area as you become more aware of all of your preparational needs.

139

The exercises here cover a variety of ego areas. Invent your own exercises. Fashion your own tools for dealing with your ego. In order to act you must always feel that you have the right to be where you are and to do what you are doing.

C. Preparations for Vulnerability

DIALOGUE ON VULNERABILITY

Eric: You know that area I've talked to you about, separating the craft into two major categories, the impressive and the expressive?

Joan: Yes, yes.

Eric: Vulnerability definitely relates to the impressive category. Preparation for vulnerability is another area, like the Ego area, that I found, in working with actors and working as an actor myself, was very important. If ninety-eight per cent of acting is preparation, the emphasis must be put on preparation, because if you are prepared to act, then you can and if you are not prepared to act, then you can't. The exercises for vulnerability stimulate your ability to be sensitive and affected. All of the exercises in this category make you more sensitive to real and imaginary stimuli. Now that's a very important point . . . *real and imaginary* . . . because if you become more available to being affected by more things, you will increase your threshold of availability, increase your vulnerability on a day-to-day living level and on a here-and-now acting level. Do you know what I mean? Do you know what I mean?

Joan: I sure do.

Eric: If you get more vulnerable as the days go by, you are affected by more existing things that were always there. And also, as you become more sensitive and affectable and vulnerable, you are affected by the imaginary things which you suggest, create or work for. So vulnerability is a monster of an important area in your preparation, because it makes you ready to be affected. For example, in class last night, you remember? I was talking to Lori and I said to her you must first get to the stage of vulnerability and surrender it before you can play an uptight bitch, and she understood that. A lot of actresses wouldn't understand that. They would start right away to work for the end result, the uptight bitch, closing all the doors.

Joan: That's right. The uptight bitch might be uptight because she's afraid of her vulnerability underneath. You gotta get that. You gotta find out what's underneath the uptight thing on top. Another thing is that this area of vulnerability is particularly embarrassing for actors to work on, because it feels squishy. It feels naked and unacty. It feels defenseless. And there's that traditional thing about the "professional," you know—you go in and say your jokes and you get your money. And even some sophisticated actors, who are sensitive people, do not allow themselves to be vulnerable on the set, on the job. It can be risky and they'd rather keep control of themselves, because they think that is what a professional is. When an actor really works in this area of vulnerability, he's not going to look professional in that slick sense of the word. He's going to look rough and bumpy.

Eric: Yeah, sometimes the red balls are all rolling in one direction and you're the white ball rolling the other way. You're a target, but you've got to do the work you *have* to do in order to do the kind of work you *want* to do. The results of your work on vulnerability, the results in terms of your *performance,* will far surpass the results of the conventional actor who says his jokes. They may laugh at you on the set or be embarrassed for you, avoid you even, but when they see your work on the screen, the laughing stops. So be the white ball and keep rolling in the direction your preparation takes you.

Joan: Right! Absolutely.

Eric: I want to say one other thing. Last night in class, Joy said to me, "I don't *want* to feel. I don't *want* to be affected. I don't want to go *through* it!" It's true, it's uncomfortable, sometimes painful. As you grow and feel more, it is very threatening, very intimidating, especially if your conditioning has been to protect yourself against feeling. But as I said to Joy last night and again and again, it's the truth, you gotta go through the thickest part of the woods in order to get out of the woods. You can stand, looking into the woods all your life and never go through them and never get to the other side. This applies to *any* area, not just vulnerability.

Joan: Wait a minute. If you're going to be a bank teller, then it's okay to look through the woods and not go through them.

Eric: I don't know. My feeling is that I think you can enjoy life more by functioning in terms of what you really feel, all your sensitivities, even if you're a bank teller.

Joan: But with an actor it's mandatory.

Eric: I don't think a bank teller's livelihood depends on it as an actor's does. However, opening up, being vulnerable and experiencing life on a higher and fuller level is better for everybody, whatever you do.

24. Group Vulnerability

Vulnerability means being open to all kinds of emotions, not just the serious, sad things or the things you're ashamed to expose, but also the frivolous feelings, the areas of fun and humor. There are two ways to do the Group Vulnerability. One individual in the group can talk about an experience that happened to him or her, sharing that experience with the group. It should be an experience that is filled with strong emotional impulses and hopefully the group will identify with that vulnerability and as more individuals share their experiences, the atmosphere in the room becomes progressively more sensitive and affectable. This is an excellent exercise for either a classroom or a rehearsal, because it makes the group ready to go on either to more preparational exercises or to dealing with the responsibilities in a piece of material. When it's done in a professional rehearsal setting, it helps if the director leads off with a vulnerable experience of his own, modeling a willingness to be open.

Another way is to have the group work by themselves simultaneously and individually. Each person works privately for his own choices and the vulnerable responses are infectious, like laughter or tears. The emotion in the room has a snowball effect, feeding on itself and promoting a higher degree of vulnerability.

25. Pique and Expose Needs

You can do a semi-audible monologue to yourself expressing your needs. "What do I need? Well, I need to work more often. I need more money. I need to have some of the things I've always wanted. I want not to be alone anymore. I wish I had more hair. I want to be thinner. I wish I knew if I were going to succeed . . . " The needs you express will kick off other areas of vulnerability. For instance, not having some of the material things you've always wanted might make you very sad. And besides pathos you might also find some humor in your needs.

Another way to pique and expose needs is to work for a stimulus, objects which represent needs, a place you've been in and long for, a person you don't see anymore but are still in love with, a fur coat you can't afford, your dream car. Working for these kinds of things should produce a chain reaction leading to other vulnerabilities.

Another way is to express out loud to another person or to a group all the things you need, including what you need from them. "I really need to be good in this play. I need to feel that everybody here likes me and accepts me. I want you to think I'm talented. I need to feel important here." You can also include any one-to-one feelings of need toward anyone in the group.

The hope is that if you truly pique your needs, whatever they are, they will give way to all the other areas of vulnerability surrounding each need. When you deal with the nucleus of something, the related parts of it become available to you and your vulnerability takes on complex dimension.

26. Evocative Words

This exercise came out of a happy accident, as many exercises have. I was working with an actress named Carey. She was sitting on the stage doing an individual exercise. I'd asked her to tell us about a meaningful experience in hopes of her being emotionally affected. She started talking about something that happened to her in school. As I watched her, I saw that she was reporting the experience and her obligation to be understood by us was taking precedence over the impact of the story on her. I stopped her and said, "Don't tell us the story, Carey. Just say single words that relate to the experience." She started saying words connected to that time and that place. After just a few words, she became affected emotionally. As she continued saying words, the emotional life was fuller and fuller. So I started experimenting with other actors and found this exercise very useful and successful.

You can do it by yourself or in front of a group. You can do it anywhere at any time. It's a marvelous exercise because you can use it in many ways—for vulnerability, for a preparation before going on stage to get into the right mood, or as a specific choice in a scene. Think of an experience in your life that was very meaningful. Start recalling the experience verbally by saying words related to that time and place and all the elements involved, such as the people, what they were wearing, the object around, sounds, weather. Say the single words or brief phrases audibly or semi-audibly. For instance, something happened to you in a park. You met with someone you loved and you were full of hope about the relationship, but the other person wanted to end it and you were shocked and deeply hurt. You might start by saying, "Park. Bench. The trees around me. Children playing. Carousel music. Balloon. Excitement. Blue sky. He's coming. Blond. Graduation ring. Damp ground. Serious eyes. Hi. Love you. No. Please. Don't say that. No sound. Lost. Sitting on the bench. Alone. Late. Cold . . . "

If you're pleased with the level of vulnerability you feel, fine. If you want to achieve a higher level of it, go on to another experience and repeat the process. It does not have to be the same kind of experience. It can be something fun or nostalgic.

Besides its preparational value, you can use this exercise as a choice in a scene to fulfill the emotional obligation of the material. By saying meaningful words to yourself in between the lines, you can stimulate the emotional life required by that section of the play.

27. Sensory Choice

Simply work for a choice through the use of sense memory, using an object which stimulates in you a high degree of emotional vulnerability.

28. Affection, Tenderness and Love

Express verbally your feelings of affection, tenderness and love toward the people in your group. It can be done in a classroom group, a rehearsal gathering or on a film set with the people around you, who don't necessarily have to know that you're doing this exercise. Look around the room and find the things that exist which really make you feel affectionate and tender, and start there. Express your feelings audibly or semi-audibly, whichever the situation dictates. "I really like you, John. I feel tremendous affection for you and I'm very attracted to you. Carol, your being here means a lot to me. I feel you're really supportive of me and encouraging." You can expand the expression of your tenderness and love to things outside of the group, people in your personal life. "I'm so in love with Mark. Last night in the restaurant his eyes were full of concern for me. And I adore my children. I'm overwhelmed with feeling when I see them. And my dog—oh, my dog, I'm crazy about my dog. He's so cute." The exercise stimulates internally the feelings of affection, tenderness and love which lead to a level of vulnerability.

29.   Fear, Love and Hate

You can do it semi-audibly, but it's better if you do it out loud to a group or another person. Talk about your fears and the things you love and hate, tossing them all together like an emotional salad. In this exercise you're not committed to just your fears or your loves or hates. You can mix them around. Be sure you take responsibility for expressing what you feel about each thing rather than just reporting. And ultimately you will pique meaningful emotional responses to things that are deeply important in your life.

30.   Ask For Help

There are two ways to do this one. The first way is simply to say, "Help me. Please help me." Repeat the phrase over and over, either alone or preferably to a group, until that one phrase reaches down into you and touches your needs. The second way is to ask for some specific kind of help related to a real need. "Would you please help me overcome my laziness? Would you call me every day and make sure I'm rehearsing? Would you help me by telling me when I'm hostile, because I don't know when I am and I really need not to be."

31.   Imaginary Monologue

I started using the Imaginary Monologue about eleven years ago, but at first I called it the Steering Wheel Monologue, because I used to do it driving my car. I'd drive along and I'd always be telling people off, having imaginary confrontations demanding what was rightfully mine or I'd tell someone how much I really cared, pouring out affection that in reality would be embarrassing to us both.

145

I introduced it to the class after I'd discovered something about myself—that I did not have to face the consequences of the other person's being there, and that it always stimulated in me some kind of emotional life.

Talk to someone who is not here now as if that person were really here, talking about things that would be either difficult or impossible for you to say if the person were really here. You will elicit meaningful, gut-level kinds of emotional investments in your relationship to the imaginary person.

Imaginary Monologue can serve many purposes. You can use it to stimulate any kind of emotional response you want as a choice in a scene or as a preparation before a scene. If you're doing it for *vulnerability,* stress the areas that are emotionally meaningful to you, creatively leading yourself into places that stimulate in you a high degree of vulnerability. You can talk to somebody you're in love with or somebody who is dead, a parent or grandparent or any significant person.

32. Abandonment Exercises for Vulnerability

The Abandonment Exercise was described in Chapter II as an antidote to tension, but this type of exercise can be used for many purposes. Because it is largely purgative, it often brings up a flow of emotionality which leaves you shaky and rumbly inside—in other words, vulnerable. You can choose from several types of Abandonment besides the basic one.

Primitive Abandonment has more form and order, because it begins with a basic primitive rhythmical beat, which you start arbitrarily, encouraging your body to move like a Watusi warrior and your throat to emit groans and percussive sounds. Allow your movements and sounds to build until you experience a kind of breakthrough, a climax of primitive release.

Mini-Abandonment is the public version of the regular Abandonment. Use it at those times when you really can't go all the way in your environment. Find a place off by yourself somewhere, in a corner, behind a flat. Do the Abandonment on a more internal level, allowing the sounds to come out, but less vocally. Tense and relax all your muscles violently, convulsively and repeatedly until the purge begins.

Flip Out is just that. Go crazy. Flamboyantly and hugely expurgate all your emotional energies, all your joy, hate, love, rage, frustration. The Flip Out is done verbally, vocally and physically.

Exorcism—Use the physical gesture of pushing away from you and vocal expressions such as Get Out! Get out of my life! Get away from me! Leave me alone! Violently rid yourself of all the people and things which are suppressing you. Sometimes you might find yourself doing battle with an abstract demon, such as Fear.

D. Preparations for the Imagination

Everybody has an imagination. Somewhere. Of some kind. Children's imaginations are available and usable, but as we grow older, things happen to us which create membranes that contain and subordinate the imagination. Because of the responsibilities of life and because our society does not encourage us to pretend and to play, even frowns on it ("That isn't adult, that's childish"), our imaginations go to sleep.

An actor's talent is very dependent on his ability to imagine. You must not only work on your imagination when you have to use it for a play or a film, but you must also work on it as part of your daily living preparations, finding all kinds of organized and unorganized exercises to stimulate it and stretch it. Start from your stretch point and go further, expanding your belief that anything is imaginatively possible. There are no boundaries. Within reality there are boundaries, but you don't have boundaries to your imagination and you shouldn't make any.

The work you do every day of your life, the day after day living preparation we've talked about at the beginning of this chapter, must include preparations for your imagination. They must go hand-in-hand with all the other kinds, the Ego Preparations, the sensitizing and sense memory and vulnerability. All the exercises here and the ten thousand more that you imaginatively invent should be used for stretching your imagination.

JELLYBEAN:

The Child Is Alive In All Of Us. Asleep In Some Of Us, But Alive

33. Pretend: Self and Two-People

Either by yourself or with another person, silently or out loud, pretend whatever pleases you to pretend, as a child would. Maybe you are in a forest surrounded by trees and animals and flowers. When I'm driving on the freeway coming home from work, I pretend I'm on a long trip across the country and I'm considering where I'll stop for the night. I look at fancy hotels and pretend I'm driving a Rolls Royce.

When you're working by yourself, try talking out loud and going through some physical actions to support the pretend circumstances. Do the exercise five minutes a day or as long as a whole day, actually venturing out into the real world pretending to be the rich lady, talking to real estate agents about buying this or that mansion, letting them show you the properties. Imagine how the rich lady might respond and allow your imagination to stimulate your behavior. Or be a tramp for a day, wearing smelly old clothes and hanging around the Skid Row area.

Two-People Pretend is a good preparation for a scene or to get a relationship going with another actor. It's also good just to have fun with, besides the basic purpose of stretching your imagination. Pretend anything together. For example, you're on an ocean cruise, sitting in deck chairs talking about what you'll see and do when you reach your destination. Or that you and your acting partner have been living together a long time and you're arguing about your relationship. Both actors should take the initiative to feed the reality with more and more imaginary circumstances and physical actions.

Although Pretend is not a Sense Memory Exercise, the spinning of pretense often leads to the seeing, hearing, tasting, feeling and smelling of those objects and elements that you're pretending. Pretend can even be used as a choice in a scene. Joan used it in a film where she had to gaze proudly at a ridiculous centerpiece in the middle of a dining table and say, "That's the prettiest centerpiece I've ever made!" She pretended that it was an Oscar Award and was filled with effusive joy.

34. Storytelling

Storytelling is an ancient art. People use it for the passing on of history, for sharing of wisdom and information, or for entertainment to pass the time. In my work with actors I've found several types of storytelling exhilarating to the imagination.

Make Up Weird, Outlandish Stories—Do it alone or in a group, silently, semi-audibly or out loud. "I was eating a hot dog and suddenly I heard a tiny voice, 'Please don't eat me until I tell you my story.' And that hot dog told me it had been an orphan . . . etc., etc." The less conventional the story and the more chances the teller takes, the better the exercise for the imagination. Remove all boundary lines of logic. You don't have to make sense. Start anywhere and go anywhere. The end of the story does not have to resemble the beginning or have any of those elements you started with.

Group Storytelling—With or without a moderator, a group of people spin a tale. One person begins telling a story and at an exciting point, the next person picks it up and takes it in his or her own direction. "I heard the footsteps—step by step—coming closer to the door. I was terrified. The door slowly opened and in came . . ." The next person might say, "A huge box of saltines and a glass of milk. And I knew I'd forgotten my bedtime snack . . . "

35. Essences and Abstracts

A party game. It's important in all of these imagination exercises to make them fun and game-like rather than arduous intellectual feats, because the imagination has its roots in the unconscious and will flow most freely when you are relaxed and light-hearted. The group selects one person, the Questioner, to leave the room, because the Questioner must not know who is chosen as the subject of the game. The group chooses their subject and the Questioner returns and asks questions about the person's essences and abstracts. "What kind of flower does this person have the essence of? What kind of weather? What color would this person be if he or she were an abstract color? What kind of food? What period of history? What character in history embodies the essence of this person? What kind of architecture? What kind of music? What time of day? What kind of odor? What metal? . . ." and so forth.

The Questioner continues until he thinks he can guess the subject and it's surprising how accurate he often is.

36. Frontis Exercise

The name comes from an actress named Frontis who brought it into my class. It's a group exercise and essentially non-verbal, although as it gathers momentum, sounds may come forth. One person begins it with some kind of real or abstract movement—for instance, conducting a symphony orchestra, standing up tall and moving the arms and the head like Toscanini. After a minute or two, a second person takes over the conducting movement, almost instantaneously changing it to some other form, such as a beautiful big butterfly sailing around the room. The first person sits down. After another couple of minutes, a third person takes over the butterfly and modifies it into something else. The movements can be either real or abstract. Even though they don't necessarily have to resemble something, they should not be without form and some kind of rhythm. The exercise continues in round robin style, the first person picking up the movement from the last person.

37. Fantasies

Fantasies do not have to have any kind of logic or story. They can be formless, fragments of impulses that you don't even understand yourself. They can be verbal or non-verbal or fantasy gibberish. They often engage your wish-fulfillment, your dreams and desires. Involving yourself in fantasies will endlessly enrish your imagination. Daydreaming, night dreaming, sexual fantasies, fantasizing with another person, having fantasies about everyone around you, and any other ways you find—explore your world of fantasy! Exposing yourself to the variety of other people's imagination helps to expand your own. You can use the group as a barometer to see if your imagination gets stuck, repeating the same pedestrian patterns.

Make Up Fantasy Stories about Objects Around You—Alone or in a group, looking around you, choose an object, maybe a chair in your breakfast room—and make up a fantasy story about it. "That chair belonged to a man by the name of Peter Venton. This man lived in a country village outside of London and he made that chair himself, for his father, who died before receiving it. Peter Venton got so attached to that chair he would sit in no other. He'd stroke the arms as he sat there, which is why the arms are so shiny now, and he'd talk to it. And the scrapes and scratches near the bottom are from his dragging the chair around, because he eventually got so attached to it . . . " and so on. Use any kinds of objects, animate, inanimate, outdoors, indoors. Let your imagination take you on a trip.

Tell an Exciting Story about Yourself—Alone or in a group, using facts or fiction or a combination of both, tell an experience you had (or didn't have), emphasizing all the exciting, adventuresome aspects. Enlarge the suspense, enhance the romance. This is a good ego preparation besides a stimulant to your imagination.

Look at Someone and Supply Imaginary Gaps—This one can be done alone. Choose a person anywhere you are—in a rehearsal group, a restaurant, a park—and make up a story. "That person is a circus performer and has just recently broken away from the circus and is trying to make a life in the city. He doesn't have any money and he's desperate. He's here in this place killing time while waiting to go see about a job . . . etc., etc." It's not an observation exercise or a deductive process. Just start with a person and let your imagination run wild.

38. Children's Games

Red Light, Green Light, Statues, Hide and Seek, Be Animals, Object Charades (take the form of an inanimate object such as a gas pump or pinball machine and people have to guess what you are)— these and any other children's games that call on the imagination are excellent. They loosen you up, get you to have fun, pique the child in you. Particularly good for actors who are rigid and afraid to be silly.

39. Believability

This exercise is far more than an Imagination Preparation. In fact, its roots are entwined in the very nucleus of what acting is. I've often thought that any one branch of our large tree of craft could in itself be developed into a total approach to acting. Music as a choice and all the endless selections you could use might become an entire system of work. Getting a physical sense of animals or of different people or inanimate objects could be enlarged and used exclusively as your approach. Believability is that kind of branch.

It is that important. But why put all your weight on one branch, when together they give you a more solid foundation, a more varied choice of tools toward dimensional acting?

When children pretend and play their games, they believe because they *want* to believe and so their wooden crate is a jet airplane. But often when an actor gets up on stage, he challenges his belief. He says to himself, "Well, this could never happen to me. This is really hard to believe. I'd never behave like that," instead of starting where children start.

I began the Believability as a Round Exercise, hoping that if the actors in my class repeated it weekly, they would heighten and expand their willingness to believe. If repeatedly the actor *wants* to believe, as children do, and *chooses* to believe in imaginary events and takes these events *personally,* then his willingness to believe will grow. Believing becomes a habit.

JELLYBEAN:

It Takes More Energy To Negate Belief Than It Does To Believe

After a couple of months of doing the Believability Round every week, I was aware of some significant things beginning to happen. People visiting the class during a Believability would often get very embarrassed and walk out, phoning me later to apologize and explain that they felt they didn't have a right to be there that night, when everybody was being so personal. They felt like Peeping Toms, spying on the privacies of other people. I realized they didn't understand that it was an exercise. They believed every minute of it! What a marvelous audience response to a theatrical event!

An author wrote a book after visiting the class and in the book called me all kinds of terrible things, because he believed the Believability exercise, misinterpreted the purpose of it and took as true everything that was totally untrue. The actors themselves would often get so involved in the Believability, they'd be affected long after the exercise was over. It's not unusual for an actor to storm out of class during this Round, upset by something which he knows is untrue, but belief has become stronger than knowledge. I realized that the energy of the group feeds each actor's willingness to believe. One person's belief stimulates another's. Twenty people feeding the imaginary circumstances eliminates that line between hypothetical and real until the air is charged with excitement. Both actors and audience reach a point where they cannot separate the truth from the untruth. Belief and disbelief get confused in a mesh of possible truths. Pretty soon you find yourself believing everything. The point is that a good Believability exercise is good theatre. The actors are unpredictable and extremely exciting to watch. There is reality in everything that's happening and that's what acting should always be.

But I saw that actors who were capable of total belief in this exercise were still having difficulty creating realities in their scene work. If you sit in a Believability Round and you're exciting and affectable and unpredictable and then you get up on a stage in a scene and you're not any of those things, it's because you haven't dealt with the obstacles between you and your belief. What you can do in a Round or in Two-People Believability you can also do in a scene, if you eliminate the obstacles to your willingness to believe and function in terms of that believed situation. Some of these obstacles are the obligation you feel to the material, your need to be "good," your need to feel a specific emotional response, emotional and intellectual concepts of all kinds, the value judgments you put on different emotions and so forth. Your choice to believe can overcome all these obstacles at once. Of course, you can shore up and support your Believability with other craft elements such as sense memory choices (the greatest Believability exercise in the world is a Sense Memory Exercise), use of available stimuli, suggestions of all kinds, and so on. But if you start with the Believability, you're halfway down the road.

You're given a set of hypothetical circumstances—Hedda Gabler, for instance. You're not married to this man. This is not your home. This is a stage set. We're in Hollywood and not in Sweden and you're not fascinated by guns. As a matter of fact you hate guns and have never owned one. Those are a set of circumstantial lies. So what you do through the craft is to substitute these lies with your own realities. But you've got to believe the existence of your own imaginary realities before you can function. The Believability exercise trains you to do that.

153

A sense memory choice is a way to create your own reality on the stage. You can create a room that is personal to you other than the stage set, a room which makes you feel as much at home there as Hedda feels in her own house. Believability exists as a part of sensory process, because you must be able to believe that you see, hear, feel, taste and smell something which actually is not there. However, Believability also allows you to believe just by the decision to believe. You can hold the gun in your hand and simply choose to believe that this object can and will end your life. The success you have in sensorily creating your room will support your belief in the deadliness of the gun. This does not mean that you must first create a reality sensorily in order to stimulate your belief by a simple decision. You may just as simply believe you're in your own room. The craft processes are only designed to support your belief.

Start the Believability exercise in a Round, mixing truth with untruths. A person might say to another person, "I waited for you until ten o'clock this morning, Tom. You didn't answer your phone." And of course, it isn't true, but Tom is obligated to respond in some way and he might say, "What are you talking about? We didn't have a rehearsal this morning." And then the first person might reply, "You mean you forgot? You're always doing that, Tom. Why do you do that? Don't you care?" Or Tom's first response might be something like, "Well, you know, I hate to say this, but I overslept. I heard the phone ringing, and I knew it was you but I was afraid to answer because I was afraid you'd be mad at me, like you are now."

A Believability exercise can start with a total untruth directed at another person, such as that one about the rehearsal. Or you can start with something untrue about yourself, a story you tell about yourself which the other people might get drawn into believing. For example, you might say, "I feel very reluctant—uh—I know this isn't a Reluctancy exercise—but I'm reluctant to say this on my last night in class. I'm going to New York in the morning and— uh—boy, I hate to say anything because I'm so excited inside I'm busting, but I got a lead in a Broadway show." Then people congratulate you. "That's fantastic! . . . What play? . . . Who's the director? . . . I told you that would happen if you'd just stick with it . . . " Somebody else might burst into tears and confess jealousy of your good fortune and even admit she's always hated you because you always get the good things. Her explosion might evoke chiding responses from some of the people and others might confess that they too had always been jealous of you.

154

Or you can start with a truth and gradually weave into it some un-truths. "You know, when you and I had coffee last week after class and we got into that big, heavy talk, I thought about it all week." Now you may actually have had coffee with that person last week, and you may have gotten into a big discussion, but now you can take that truth into an entirely fictitious area. You use the truth as a springboard and then people can bandwagon and either challenge or supplement the elements of what you're talking about. Someone might say, "I don't believe that. I don't believe a word you're say-ing." And instead of this criticism stopping the flow of the exercise, it can be used as part of the Believability. You can answer, "That's what's wrong with you, Jean. You never believe anything." And the others can bandwagon and support your accusation.

All the people in the Round can jump in and build something that one person starts. Or if one person is encountering another, people can take sides or start a one-to-one confict with that person, saying something like, "Hey, I've noticed that about you, Joe. You do things like that. What she said about you is true. You've been like that with me." And that could either be true, semi-true or not true at all. The exercise builds and grows in momentum of belief.

There's a certain trap to avoid in the Believability Round. The exer-cise has a tendency to get conflict-ridden, negative and hostile, mainly because in encountering another person, people choose areas of conflict which are often negative in order to get something going and to elicit an immediate response from another person. That's a trap, leading to an overload of negativity in the group. It is not only depressing but can sometimes take the place of more tender and vulnerable areas, areas which are really harder to expose because they're often more frightening. To avoid this trap, encourage your-self to bring in as many positives as negatives. "Joan, I love you. I've always loved you. It's hard for me to admit that to you, but I really love you." And then Joan might reply,? "I've often felt that from you, but it embarrasses me and I don't know how to handle it." Now that positive exchange can be partially true or not true at all, and that positivity can build on another and another.

The dialogues may either run themselves out to a conclusion or some other person may start a whole new thing in the middle. For example, the dialogue about the rehearsal . . . "Tom, you didn't show up for rehearsal this morning. You didn't answer your phone." And Tom says, "I'm sorry, I overslept," etc. Then somebody else might say to someone, "You know that coat you bought for me? It was stolen out of my apartment." Of course these statements come one at a time, because if everybody talks at once, it's mayhem. But various dialogues can interweave. The two people who started with the rehearsal argument may go back to it later in the exercise and take it further into deeper, more personal areas. There is no clear-cut form. You may bandwagon on a dialogue or disregard it and start your own.

John Fiorito begins a Believability with Flo. "Flo, last night when I was over at your house for dinner, I was hurt by you. You hurt my feelings. You were cold and detached and uncommunicative. And when I got home it was hard to go to sleep, because I really felt hurt." Flo might say, "I'm sorry, John. It wasn't intentional. I had a bad week." John might continue with, "I think you do that a lot with me. I think you take advantage of the fact that you know how I feel about you. You use it. You manipulate me and I think you get something out of it." Flo might come back with, "John, are you going to start that paranoid crap with me? I don't take advantage of anything. I just had a bad week, a bad month, a bad year, John."

Now John may not have been there for dinner last night or ever, but he may have chosen to start the Believability with Flo because he has, in truth, a real attraction to her which is not returned. He chooses to work in an area which has its seeds in a personal truth. By the same token, Flo might really have had "a bad day, a bad month, a bad year," as she says to John. She may actually, at this moment, be filled with despair about her life. In this instance, the facts aren't true, but the feelings are.

Instead of just sitting there and listening to Flo and John, which you're allowed to do if you want, you might jump in and say, "Yeah, John, you have a tendency to get hurt very easily. You imagine hurts that aren't there. Last week when I walked into class and you said I didn't say hello to you, it's because I didn't *see* you, John, and that's the truth." Then John might defend himself and say, "You walked right by me. You looked at me and snubbed me, man. Don't give me any of that crap, because you did." Then he might go on with Flo.

Sometimes, after starting a Believability exercise, you forget that it's an exercise. One night in the Round, David said he wanted to share something with the class. He said that he and Leigh, a girl in the class, were engaged to be married. Everyone was surprised and elated. "Gee, how long has this been going on? . . . That's wonderful! . . ." etc., etc. He explained they'd kept it a secret because they didn't want everybody talking about it before they'd made their decision. People congratulated them and I thought to myself, "Gee, that's really nice. They'll make a nice couple." Leigh was glowing. She blushed and there were tears in her eyes as she talked about their future together. A week later I was sitting out by my pool taking some sun and I got this warm glow, a feeling for David and Leigh. I thought, "Gee, isn't that nice how people meet in my class and some of them get married." I felt personally responsible for the match and I got very involved in this good feeling about it and then suddenly I realized it happened in a Believability exercise. It wasn't true. It never was true. And it isn't true now. I felt I'd been had. But it proved to me my desire to believe was so strong that even though I knew somewhere it wasn't true, the seed of belief grew and lived a whole week.

As you participate in a Believability Round over a period of time, keep pushing your line of believability further and further away by gradually making things harder and harder to believe. Be aware when something is impossible for you to believe and try to find out why. If you can define what makes you doubt your belief, then maybe there's a way you can deal with that, some adjustment you can make that helps you to believe. Ask yourself what seed of truth exists that could hook you into the lie. Next time when this same kind of untruth comes up, you'll be more ready to believe it and able to make the adjustment on your feet rather than after the fact. Limits of believability vary from actor to actor. Get to know your own personal limits and keep stretching them. Keep lowering your Threshold of Believability. *As you become more able to believe in anything, you become more able to believe in everything.*

Believability exercises—the Round, Two-People and One-Person— are great for your imagination, since the imagination is constantly called upon in these exercises. You can also use Believability as a choice in a scene by simply choosing to believe that this is a room out of your life, this woman is your mother, that suitcase is really full of ransom money. Or you can use Believability to supplement another choice because belief is implicit in the success of any choice. Besides all these uses, Believability is a root training exercise that must become part of your whole approach to acting. The threads of it should run through every exercise you do.

JELLYBEAN:

It Is As Easy To Believe
As It Is To Disbelieve

II. PREPARATIONS FOR RELATING TO PEOPLE, OBJECTS AND PLACES

In this section, as before, preparation means preparing to act, to do a scene in a film or a play. Getting related to the other actor is very important, because most acting occurs between two or more people. Getting related to the place and objects in it is also imporant, because every time you act, what you do and how you do it depends on *where* you do it. The place and what it means to you affects your character in the scene. The writer purposely sets the action of a scene in a particular place because that place has something to do with what's going on and has a specific influence on the people in the scene. For example, I would behave differently having a domestic argument on the corner of Hollywood and Vine than I would in my own bedroom. My voice would be different. My relationship to the other person would be distracted by passers-by. My sense of privacy would be distracted.

The following sequence begins with exercises for getting related to the other actor, but that doesn't mean you must start there before you work on the place and objects. Start with whatever is necessary. In some scenes the relationship between the two characters may be far more significant than their relation to the place. In an all-consuming love affair, for instance, the lovers are more important to each other than any of the places they're in. In this case, you would prepare for your relationship to your partner first and enrich it later by creating the place. In other scenes it's the other way around—the place is more important than the actor's relationship, or equally so.

158

40. Two-People Believability

This is done the same way it is done in the Believability Round. Either person can start or they can start simultaneously. The exercise can be used simply to heighten your willingness to believe or you can choose to lead yourself into an area of believability which parallels the circumstances of the material.

Excerpt from a class tape, January, 1973:

Ruth: She had me almost believing what I—I—but I *knew* what was in my locket!

Joan: The line of believing that you speak of, Eric, occurred for me at the very beginning, the very first lie I told I was aware of its being a lie and I took a deep breath and some little echo of the past said, "Oh now, Joanie, don't lie." You know, some little mother's governessy voice. And I took a deep breath and said a very simple easy thing, a simple ordinary untruth and once I got over that hump, Eric, my believability increased and I got so bizarre. I got hold of this locket and I believed that there were baby's toenails in it.

Eric: You mean, like it was an occult talisman?

Joan: I believed it! I believed that this witch—that she had a pressed embryo in there and . . .

Ruth: I *knew* that it had my husband's picture in there, but she made me feel really creepy about it.

Eric: Joan's believability kicked off Ruth's believability that there was something strange and mystical about that locket when, in fact, Ruth, you feel very warm about that locket and knew all the time what was in it. But Joan made you doubt and feel differently about your locket. Therefore, the two of you, starting with an untruth, a lie, were able to create an emotional life together based on that lie which you chose to believe.

41. Blind Investigate

Two actors close their eyes and investigate each other with their other four senses. They touch each other's faces, arms, bodies. They smell, taste, listen. The purpose of this kind of investigation is to take much less for granted. Our eyes lead us to taking things for granted and when sight is denied, you become much more sensorily related and involved and in tune with the other person. From that point of involvement you are then much readier to work with your partner toward dealing with the material, because you are sensorily related.

42. Observe, Wonder and Perceive

Refer to Chapter II under Observe, Wonder and Perceive II. This exercise definitely gets you related to the other actor. You can do it with or without the other actor's knowing it.

Two actors talk to each other, expressing moment-to-moment their fears in relation to each other.

Michelle:	I'm afraid to say the first line.
Charles:	Me too. I'm glad you have the first line. And I'm afraid you don't like me.
Michelle:	That's nonsense, Charles. I don't dislike you at all. I like you.
Charles:	I'm afraid of this material. I don't think I can do it.
Michelle:	It scares me too. And I'm afraid of you, because you've had much more experience than I've had.
Charles:	Maybe so, but I'm afraid to be here, because I'm afraid of what will or won't happen . . . etc.

43. Talk About What You're Most Afraid Of

The expression of fears between two people often eliminates obstacles that would ordinarily plague the rehearsal process. Things that fester, hidden away, keep you from your own vulnerability.

44. Non-Verbal Communication

You relate to your partner without words. You may use sounds and gibberish and physical movements. Start by relating to what is going on at the moment between the two of you. The exercise encourages a communication which is not dependent on the meaning and understanding of words. It elicits more visceral, emotional responses instead of a cerebral, verbal rapport.

45. Relate Moment-to-Moment with What You Feel

Two people relate to each other verbally and non-verbally in a stream-of-consciousness form, expressing moment-to-moment everything that's going on individually and between them. Include in your conversation all those thoughts and impulses that have nothing to do with the other person, such as sounds outside, your awareness of being here and looking for things to talk about, besides those impulses and feelings you have toward the other person. This preparation trains you to include everything so that you don't have to function in spite of anything, right from the very beginning of a two-people relationship.

46. Share

Share with each other those things which are personally meaningful to you. It can be about anything in any area. The purpose of sharing meaningful things is that it gets you closer to each other, more involved and caring. If, as people, you feel for each other, then, as actors, you start with that level of feeling and carry it into the material.

47. Two-People Trick

This preparation is used primarily as an antidote to premeditated acting, because it keeps both actors in a state where they don't know what's coming next. It can be done while they're saying the lines of the scene or while they're improvising on the scene or during a Believability or really any kind of communication exercise, verbal or non-verbal. They both can agree to do it or one actor can decide to do it without the other's knowledge or permission. Either actor suddenly does or says something unexpectedly, often large or bizarre things, sometimes conventional things, but always unexpected. The other actor must respond impulsively to how the trick affected him and include his impulsive reaction in the relationship.

For example, two people are calmly talking together about what a nice day it is and suddenly one of them jumps up and starts screaming or doing an Abandonment exercise. The other actor is obligated to respond to however that truly makes him feel, whether or not those feelings have any logical connection to what they were talking about. A more subtle example might be in a love scene, when the two actors are exchanging passionate lines and caresses. At any point one of the actors might become cold and detached, withdrawing from the partner while still mouthing the passionate words of the material. The other one then must deal with how that withdrawal really makes him feel, rather than clinging to his concept of the scene.

The purpose of the Two-People Trick is to encourage both actors to trust their impulses in responding to each other. The more they trust, the more impulsive their relationship will be, not only within the exercise or the improvisation, but also within the scene. Actors commonly hold concepts about how a scene should go or how a character would or would not behave, and these concepts are usually restrictive and narrow. As a result, the acting comes out smoothly, perhaps competently, but conventionally. It's amazing how the work takes on many surprisingly unique and human colors when actors find out how many different kinds of behavior fit into any given scene. Besides its use as a preparation for getting related to the other actor, the Trick exercise can be used in rehearsals and in performances to avoid being predictable and premeditated.

48. Imaginary Monologue to a Real Partner but Talking to Someone Else

The instructions for Imaginary Monologue appear earlier in this chapter. In the exercise here you talk to the other actor, but the things you're saying are things you're saying to your father or wife or whomever you've chosen to talk to. In the usual Imaginary Monologue you're talking to someone who is not there. You're speaking to an empty chair. Now in this exercise the other actor *exists* and the fact that he's there and responding to what you're saying gives your Imaginary Monologue a very different dimension. You are provoking responses from the other actor which may or may not be similar to the behavior of your father or wife and this leads to an unpredictable relationship. The other actor and your imaginary person meld into one and hopefully take you to the desired emotional life.

49. Imaginary Dialogue with Real Partner, Take Personally What's Said to You

Do this the same way you do the Imaginary Monologue to a Real Partner, except in this exercise both actors are talking to imaginary people and you choose to take personally whatever the other actor says to you. The value of it is that both people are responding to real and imaginary stimuli at the same time. There are elements of Believability and also elements of the Trick exercise, because it's impossible for the other actor to behave as your imagined person would and you have to deal with these constant surprises in his behavior. It makes for a very exciting two-people preparation.

50. Pick Up on Everything You Didn't Notice Before

You can use this exercise either for getting related to the other actor or for getting related to the place and objects. As the name suggests, you decide to notice all those things about the person or the place that you never noticed before. What color are her eyes? How long is her neck? You may never have observed how tall she is. How many windows in this room? What things are hanging on the walls?

51. Make Yourself Comfortable in This Place

You've come into a strange place, a rehearsal room, the stage at a first rehearsal, an office waiting room. Begin by asking yourself "How can I make myself comfortable in this place?" You might choose to do the exercise by becoming involved in what really exists, first acknowledging your discomfort and then observing and perceiving the objects in the room, which gets you out of yourself and related to the place. Another way is to use the sense memory process to create familiar objects which, if they really were in this place, would make you feel comfortable and secure.

52. Build a Beautiful Place Around You

This is a Sense Memory Exercise, which you use to build a place that is more creatively stimulating than the place you're in. For instance, you can change a drab sound stage into a beautiful Hawaiian beach or to a forested mountaintop.

53. Sensory Speculation

The exercise has several purposes. It's a sense memory practice, an additional Sensitizing exercise and a way to get you more related to the place you're in and to the person you're working with. You ask speculative questions. What would it feel like to touch that wall over there? What would the texture feel like on the tips of my fingers? You're asking these questions from a distance away and you respond in your fingertips to what you sensorily imagine. Then you walk over to the wall and feel it, finding out how close your speculation was to the real wall on your fingertips. What would that ashtray smell like? Try to imagine in your nose the component parts of that odor. Maybe you see that there are old butts and gum wrappers in the ashtray. Sensorily speculate on all those elements and then walk over and relate to the real object. Choose objects that engage all five senses. Give your senses a real workout. You can do Sensory Speculation with a person too.

54. Affecting How You Already Feel

This is one of the most important areas of preparation. In order to get to where you want to go in a scene, you have to know where you are now. Let's say you've done all your preparations for getting ready to act. You've done your relaxation exercises, your Sensitizing and Personal Inventories and now you're ready, but you want to feel something other than what you're feeling now, because you know that's the obligation in the material. Often this intermediate step is overlooked.

The actor jumps from a general preparedness to a specific obligation without building a bridge in between. Even the most seasoned actor can fall into this chasm. He feels good, he's ready to act and he starts to work for his choice in the scene. But that choice he's working for may be very hard to come to because of the way he's feeling. He's excited and turned on to acting and creative, but the person he's playing in the scene is very shy, tender and vulnerable. It's difficult to go from excitement to shyness without some interim steps. When he tries to make this jump, he's often disappointed that his choice doesn't work as well as he expected. He says, "Last night in the theatre I used this choice and it took me on a trip. It was wonderful! Tonight I went on stage and worked for the same choice and —nothing. Nothing happened." Some actors are totally confused by that. They feel the choice is no good anymore and they discard it.

But it's not the choice. The way he felt last night was very conducive to his being affected by that choice. And the way he is feeling tonight is subtlely different, but different enough so that he is not as easily affected by that same choice. He's a little more insulated tonight and protective. He had an argument with someone and the echoes of it are still rumbling around inside on a less than conscious level. On the surface he's not aware of a great difference between last night and tonight, but because he did not do his Personal Inventories and find out how he really feels, he can't relate to the differences. And those subtle things are enough to keep his choices from working.

If he did a Personal Inventory, maybe he'd find out that he has residual resentments from that argument and these unexpurgated emotions are preventing him from being affected by his choice. Once he identifies his obstacles through Personal Inventory, then his course is clear. He must choose an interim preparation to expurgate those residual feelings. He might do a Vesuvius or have an Imaginary Monologue with the person saying all the things he couldn't say this afternoon, or an Abandonment or Dump or any number of large expressive exercises, thereby freeing himself of those trapped impulses that keep him from functioning. But before he can do any kind of interim preparation, he must first know what's going on inside.

After doing your general preparations, find out how you feel. Then you might try your choice as a way of taking your emotional temperature. If the choice works, you're ready. If it doesn't, go back to your Personal Inventory and locate the obstacles. You might need some kind of interim bridge. Affecting how you already feel is a very important part of preparing, not only because it changes what is to what you want in the scene, but also because it enables you to repeat your work.

After finding out *how you feel* through Personal Inventory or any number of other exercises (sometimes you're so insulated that Personal Inventory doesn't reveal much to you and you have to get into larger, more freeing exercises), then find out *how you want to feel* by *identifying the obligation* in the material. The obligation is that emotional life that you want to experience. What do you want to feel about the other person in the scene? What do you want to feel about the place? What does your character feel generally, conglomeratively. There are thematic obligations, time obligations and many other kinds, but most often your first concern is your relationship to the other person. Find out specifically how you want to feel in that relationship and then find out where you are in your present moment-to-moment life. Then you will have some ideas about what you can do to go from one state of BEING to another.

55. Affecting the Way You Feel About the Other Actor

1. How do I feel about him (her) here and how?

2. How do I want to feel about him (her) in the scene?

3. What Availabilities can I use?

4. Isolate and emphasize the Availabilities.

5. Endowment—a sensory choice.

This series of questions is a preparation I found as an actor and in helping other actors. You can use it under fire and on your feet. It really works. It's a list of things you ask yourself in a beginning rehearsal when you start a scene. First you ask yourself, "How do I feel about that actor (actress)? How do I feel about her right here and now?" Take a kind of Personal Inventory about what you see, hear, taste, smell and feel in relation to that particular actress. You might say to yourself, "Well, she's all right. She doesn't thrill me to death. She's an interesting looking woman. She's got pretty hair. Pretty eyes. I like her. I don't dislike her. I don't feel any strong, important emotional feelings about her. I feel kind of a neutral feeling. I guess if I got to know her, I might feel other things. I don't know anything about her. She's kind of bland, actually . . ."

Once you've taken that kind of inventory and really know how you feel about her, then ask yourself, "How do I want to feel about her in the scene?" You've read the scene and you understand what the author wants and you identify your obligation. In this case, maybe the author wants you to feel extremely excited about the girl, sparks flying between you, an electricity about this woman that attracts you powerfully on every level, sexual, emotional, intellectual. That's a very different state than what you feel about her now.

The third step you take, after you've found out how you feel and defined how you want to feel and discovered that they're poles apart, is to ask yourself the question, "What is available? What is there existing in this actress that I can use to stimulate the feelings I want?" You really look the person over from head to toe, not just visually, but using all your senses to explore all the Availabilities that might appeal to you. A sound in her voice, a scent, an odor, the shape of her breasts, the way she moves, something you see behind her eyes, what her hair and skin feel like, how she clasps your hand. Once you've found several things which are *there*, several Availabilities, then the next step is to isolate those elements one at a time and emphasize your relationship to each one. For instance, maybe her mouth reminds you of someone you were once in love with and looking at her mouth rekindles unconscious responses to a love affair you had five years ago. One at a time emphasize your relationship to each Availability by not only looking at it, but relating to it with all your senses, asking yourself questions, smelling, listening, touching. Emphasis does not mean exclusion of the total person. While you are using the one Availability, you continue to relate to the total person. You hope that the Availabilities will take you where you want to go, but even if they don't, they will start you in the right direction. They will start you off in the area of excitement and attraction.

After you've exhausted all that is available (in some cases that will be enough) and you find yourself closer to how you want to feel about her, but still no sparks, then you must go on to the next step, which is Endowment. Endowment is a sensory process. You create sensory elements related to an object, in this instance, a person. You endow your partner with physical attributes, emotional attributes, vocal behavior and intellectual attitudes that appeal to you, things which you know if they really existed in this actress would excite you. You might create a look in her eyes, endow her with intelligence that manifests itself in some sensory way, bathe her in exotic scents, give her longer eyelashes. You can work to create her naked and endow her with exciting sexual odors. Whatever you choose to endow her with, you do it through the sense memory process. It is not done through suggestion.

56. Preparational Inventories

What kind of preparations do I need? This is a question you ask yourself repeatedly. Starting from your general preparations, which include your Personal Inventory, and on through your identification of the demands in the material and the changes you make in how you feel about the other actor, you are constantly taking Preparational Inventories. What kind of preparations do I need to take me where I want to go?

Preparational Inventory is similar to Personal Inventory, except that it focuses much more specifically on your feelings as they relate to the obligation and on your knowledge of what kinds of preparations are available to you and how they work for you. Your growing experience is important here. Having worked with many preparations, many kinds of choices, your experience will give you the ability to know what they did for you. Gradually you will catalogue your personal repertoire of preparational choices.

57. Create a Different Environment

Where you are has a great deal to do with the way you behave. Changing your environment will change how you feel. You can create a different environment through several ways: sense memory, isolation and emphasis, endowment, suggestion, pretending, bringing with you real objects that are personally meaningful. You're in a park and there's a lot of litter around you and it's a drab day and you want to be filled with the joy of nature and life. Through isolation and emphasis you can use that beautiful tree in front of you, relating only to the tree and to the green patch of grass beneath it. Hopefully you will stimulate a sense of being close to nature in a joyous environment. Or you can endow the tree with more foliage than it has, birds, sweet-smelling blossoms and put a blue sky behind it with billowing white clouds.

58. Sensory Choice To Meet Obligation

You can choose to work for an object which is not really here. Object, of course, means anything inanimate, animate, a person, a sound, a piece of music, a photograph, a texture, part of a place, a letter, an odor—anything that once created sensorily will affect you the way you want to be affected.

59. Make Everything Around You More Important Than You

You choose to make everything around you more important to you than you. You can fulfill the choice through a simple involvement by asking questions that aren't necessarily sensory. Where did that piece of furniture come from? I wonder who it belongs to and what period it is. Is it an original or a copy?

Or you can ask what-if questions, sensorily speculating about the things around you. Or through the sensory process you can modify the objects, giving them different colors, textures, shapes, creating a person in the chair, anything that makes the place more interesting. You can Pretend, Storytell, Fantasize, any approach to get you more involved in your surroundings and absorbed by them. This preparation changes your emotional life by getting you out of yourself, relating to a place outside of your own concerns.

60. Say Words to Yourself Relating to a Meaningful Experience

This is another way to change how you feel. The experience can be real or imaginary as long as it is meaningful and has impact on you. Don't tell yourself a story, because that will lead you to report rather than experience. Say single words, or short phrases while re-experiencing the event.

III. PREPARATIONS FOR DOING THE ROLE

Even though the preparation can be as complex as any of the work you do to fulfill the scene, preparation for doing the scene does not mean execution of the scene. It means getting ready to tackle the scenic obligations, understanding them and making them clear to yourself. Preparations are to prepare you for the selection and usage of choices. The more courageous your preparations are, the greater the risk of failure, but the richer your work will be at those times when you're successful. Remember, you use preparation not only to fulfill the emotional life of the material, but also to get to BEING. You can't run the race without getting ready to run.

From Joan's Journal: Using Preparation on the Job

"I arrived at Columbia Ranch having had two hours sleep last night. We shot the love scene today. It was 100 degrees in the studio. I knew with heat and lack of sleep I'd have to use my craft skillfully to get through the work. By the end of the day I realized I'd never been quite as successful as I was today in consciously employing things to help myself.

"The preparations I chose were not done parenthetically. That is, I didn't go off behind a flat to work and I didn't appear to anyone around as if I were *doing* anything special. Instead I found ways to weave the exercises into the life on the set, encountering and relating to the people in various ways and responding to their reactions. This is a big improvement for me, because I used to keep myself isolated, cloistered in my dressing room and then I'd have to cross that Big Line between the privacy of my room and getting in front of the camera to do the scene. Today I found how to mix it all together.

"The scene required me to be sensually alive and excited, really turned on to Rick. I sat in my chair while they set up the shot and did Tense and Relax, Logey, Sensitize and Personal Inventory. Found out I'm feeling depressed and anxious. A friend of mine got arrested last night and went to jail on false charges. I had to go downtown around midnight and help raise bail and get her out of Sybil Brand. Terrible place. So I did some Ego Exercises and Positivity to bring myself up and brighten my outlook. After I felt better I did Sensuality to get myself in touch with my body. Feeling numb, not sexy at all. Ten or fifteen minutes of Sensuality got the juices going. We did the master shot and Rick's close-ups and then it was lunch time.

"After lunch I went into a slump. Oppressively hot, maybe 105 degrees by now. My scalp was so wet that the hairdresser could hardly move the hair without the whole shape falling down. She did her best and then I moved to the make-up chair, but the old nanny goat refused to touch me up, because he said the director would yell at him if I was late on the set. I felt deprived. I felt I needed the touch of hands on my face to get me through the afternoon. I chose to do a Reluctancy at that point, telling the guy how unpleasant he was to work with, how unprofessional, etc. He did the touch-up. I went on the set, shaking, but expurgated and felt a lot better. Had I not done that, it would have boiled inside me, the Perpetual Nice Girl, and it would have kept me from being able to act. I was trembling from the risk I'd taken, so I did a quick Self Perspective, recalling myself five years ago, a scared and silent mouse on the set, as compared to now, asking for what is due to me. This calmed me, but I still wasn't where I'd been before lunch. So I did a Silly Dilly, bursting into operatic song and running around squawking like a chicken. Everybody laughed and that picked up my spirits.

"When it came time for my close-up, I prepared by doing an Imaginary Monologue to Larry, a gorgeous man I'd just met last Sunday. I had about half an hour to create him there and I asked to be my own stand-in so that I could work in the set. I used sense memory to create Larry. He was standing there under the lights, lanquid and seductive. I talked to him semi-audibly and he talked back to me, making me laugh and giggle and blush, which is just the behavior I wanted in the scene. I moved him over to the sofa. He sat down and crossed his long legs, winked at me suggestively. By the time they were ready to shoot I was ready to work. I did it in one take and the director was hugging me afterwards and the cameraman said I came across very sexy on camera. Self Perspective again—remember five years ago?—not sexy at all, cold and uptight on camera."

These are the preparations that Joan chose to use to meet the emotional obligations of this particular scene in this show. The preparational exercises you can choose from are numerous and the combinations are endless. You select your own cluster of preparations not only to fulfill the demands of the material but also to deal with the circumstances surrounding the execution of that day's work, which includes the weather—105 degrees, how you feel—two hours sleep, the way the director relates to you—or the make-up man, your physical state of health, your mental outlook. The circumstances around you influence your state of BEING and dictate the nature and mixture of your preparational choices. The obligations of the material remain constant, but your state of BEING is ever-changing.

Some suggested preparations:

61.   Two-People Three-Part Relationship

1.   Wonder, Perceive and Observe.

2.   Work for a sensory choice without any emotional obligation.

3.   Obligate yourself to an emotional result and work for a sensory choice.

62.   Two-People Preparation

1.   Investigate each other in all ways, verbally and sensorily.

2.   Go with what is, expressing moment-to-moment, verbally and non-verbally, everything you feel.

3.   Isolate and emphasize many parts of the person and see how each isolation makes you feel.

4.   Work for any sensory choice in relation to the other person.

5. Obligate yourself to something you want to feel in relation to the person, make a choice and work for it.

This preparation helps you be ready to work with that specific actor. It may also facilitate the obligations of the text.

63.   Group Preparation

A good workout for a rehearsal group or a class.

1. Wonder to yourself about everything in the room.

2. Wonder semi-audibly about one person.

3. Semi-audibly or out loud ask one question about each person you're curious about.

4. Two-People Observe, Wonder and Perceive. (Now the group is working in pairs and the director or teacher may decide to switch the pairs around during the following steps or keep them together.)

5. Two-People Double Exposure.

6. Two-People Fun-Love-Trick.

7. Two-People Believability.

8. Two-People Sense Memory, working with and without the real object.

64.   Pretend Series

1. Pretend by yourself. Keep it colorful and child-like.

2. Pretend with another person.

3. Pretend Sense Memory by yourself, combining Pretend with the Sense Memory process.

4. Pretend Sense Memory with another person.

65. Character Background Preparation

Good for a class or a rehearsal group or for two actors working on a scene together.

1. Each one talks in the first person about his character in the play and the others ask questions, encouraging him to fill in the gaps.

2. Each actor then works alone, sensorily creating, one at a time, the realities that lead to the fulfillment of the character. For example, your character in the play talks a lot about his physical exhaustion. You may now work to create that exhaustion.

3. Each actor chooses a scene from the play, defines an emotional obligation in that scene and works for a choice.

66. Three-Step Monologue

A preparation you do alone with a piece of dramatic material.

1. Say the text of the monologue out loud, letting the words come out of the moment-to-moment life that is going on in you.

2. Work for a choice not related to the emotional obligations in the monologue and say the text.

3. Work for a choice that hopefully fulfills an obligation in the monologue, and say the text. This preparation enables you to sneak up on a choice while training you to let the material come out of your BEING.

67. Four-Part Word Preparation

1. Say words to yourself that affect you—meaningful words out of your life but not necessarily related to a single experience.

2. Define how you want to feel and say words that you think will make you feel that way.

3. Pick an experience, not knowing how the experience will affect you, and say words related to it.

4. Two people working on a scene—say the lines to each other and say your own affecting words in between the lines.

These groups are not sacred. You can mix them up, borrow something from one, delete something else, add any of the exercises in this book and invent your own. What's really important is having your finger on your pulse, knowing whether or not you need an instrumental preparation at the moment or if you need a preparation dealing with your environment or with the other actor, or whatever. This kind of intimate knowledge about your instrument comes out of daily practice, taking Personal Inventories, Sensory inventories, doing all of those preparational exercises over a period of time so that you are aware of what works and what doesn't, and when. Failure and success are an integral part of your never-ending growth process. As you catalogue all those things you find out about yourself related to preparation, getting ready to act and, in fact, acting, you begin to get in touch with what touches you.

BEING is not just a way of working, it is a complete philosophy and a way of life. To have the luxury of being able to do what you want to do with your life, to experience who you are and what you want, to pursue your work for the sake of your own personal fulfillment and to reap the rewards of the creative process, this is what BEING affords. If you use the exercises in this book and make them a part of your life, and they become the fabric of your behavior, you will embark on a journey that leads to a never-neverland of wonderfully full living experiences. The work not only enriches your life enormously, it allows you to act on a level that is unique and rare in the theatre. You, the artist, will develop the totality of your own individual statement.

To Be Or Not To Be, That Is The Question ..... And The Answer